'The pages of this book called me back into that which we have preached around the world, yet often left undone – our first love passion for Jesus. I had to put the book down and get alone with God. Prayer is so much more than a spiritual exercise toward benefits received; it is as Charlie Cleverly describes, a "discipline of intimacy". His near and intimate Presence alone will satisfy the longing of the soul.'

John Arnott, Senior Pastor
Toronto Airport Christian Fellowship

'Every now and then there comes a time in history when things don't seem to be going the way we desire. Confusion, fear and anxiety grip our hearts and we are at a loss what to do. It is at such moments that we need to hear a clear prophetic voice pointing out the way to us. Charlie Cleverly's book is coming to the world at just such a time, and it is clearly a prophetic voice pointing to a simple, easily applicable way of prayer. It will change your life as you read it. It will bring back hope to a world that is so confused. This is recommended reading.'

Revd John Mulinde
World Trumpet Mission, Uganda

'Very moving, practical, helpful, inspiring – and impossible to put down.'

Sandy Millar, Holy Trinity Brompton

'Most of us do it, far more than we are aware of. At the same time we sense guilt as we don't do enough of it. We can become even more confused that Jesus told a group of people that they would not be heard the more because they prayed long prayers. Charlie Cleverly is a man of prayer, but he's fun and loves the church. This book will help those of us who, in our heart of hearts, don't really believe we know how to pray. Well done, Charlie! The stories and the scriptures blended together will help us to connect with heaven.'

Gerald Coates – speaker, author, broadcaster

‘In these last days the Lord has been teaching his people to pray. And in response God has graciously poured out his blessings from heaven. The Brazilian church has been learning to pray and the heavens have opened wide as millions have been brought into the kingdom of God, and corruption and injustice have increasingly come under God’s judgement. Reading this book will surely cause you to cry out to God, ‘Lord, teach your people to pray! Teach me to pray!’

Harry Scates, leader of Shalom network of churches, Uberlandia, Brazil, and member of the ‘Go to the Nations’ committee

‘This book provides us with a beautifully written, easily digestible, biblically based inspiration to press on in prayer. Charlie Cleverly offers us a timely classic.’

Bishop David Pytches

The Discipline of Intimacy

Charlie Cleverly

KINGSWAY PUBLICATIONS
EASTBOURNE

First published 2002
Reprinted 2003

ISBN 1 84291 049 3

Published by
KINGSWAY COMMUNICATIONS LTD
Lottbridge Drove, Eastbourne BN23 6NT, England.
Email: books@kingsway.co.uk

Book design and production for the publishers by
Bookprint Creative Services, P.O. Box 827, BN21 3YJ, England.
Printed in Great Britain.

This book is dedicated to
my dearly loved father
Peter Cleverly

Nunc dimittis servum tuum, Domine . . . in pace

Contents

Acknowledgements

I am deeply grateful to the members of Belleville Reformed Church, Paris. You are dear to me and I thank God for you every time I think of you. I thank God for the passionate, affectionate French believers from whom we have learnt so much. I am grateful for the chance to have served for ten years in a 'church for all nations': I think of you – believers from Lebanon, Egypt, Israel, Morocco, Cameroon, Togo, Benin, Rwanda, Nigeria, Algeria, Congo Republic, Madagascar, USA, Brazil, Columbia, Guadeloupe, Dominican Republic, Haiti, Ireland, Portugal, Britain, Germany, Switzerland, Sweden, Norway, Austria, Russia, Iran, China, Philippines, New Zealand. You are beloved in the eyes of God. Watching you worshipping God together is a foretaste of heaven.

I owe a debt of thanks to John Mulinde and to the memory of Prossy Mulinde from Kampala, Uganda. John, you have taught us so much. I thank God for you and for your friendship and your example. Prossy was a 'hidden warrior who will be remembered as a mother by thousands', and yet who went to be with Christ, which is far better, at the age of 35.

I thank also my four children and my son-in-law, who learnt to follow God in a foreign land. Thank you for your wonderful company, your laughter, your passion and your love.

Finally, heartfelt thanks to my wife, Anita, who understood how to pray long before I began to. You are ever an inspiration and a joy to me.

Foreword

Please don't say, 'What, another book on prayer?' We are all learners in this glorious and unending school. The author emphasises the essential ingredient of the life of prayer and intercession . . . intimacy with God. It is one of the sources of intimacy and also the result of intimacy.

My heart was kindled and warmed as I read the chapters, as yours will be too. Not only are the theological truths clearly stated, but also these truths have been demonstrated and proved in the author's experience in ministry, church planting and calling a nation to prayer.

Read the book and reread it. Apply its truths and teach them to somebody else, and borrow the outpouring of a praying David: 'O You Who hears prayer, to You all flesh shall come.' Having known the author and his dear wife for over twenty years, I wholeheartedly recommend this book.

Campbell McAlpine

Part 1

1

A Nostalgia for Heaven

'Then I with the multitude of my redeemed
Shall enter Heaven long absent, and return,
Father to see thy face, wherein no cloud
Of anger shall remain, but peace assured,
And reconcilement; wrath shall be no more
Thenceforth, but in thy presence joy entire.'
(John Milton)[1]

Writing a book on prayer is a perilous undertaking, for I am tempted at each moment to lay aside the project in favour of praying! Yet it is a privilege, too, as the subject is one so close to the heart of God. Indeed, I dare say that it is when we learn to pray that we meet and encounter God, and hence discover deep healing, renewal and purpose. For learning to pray is learning to be 'in touch' with the One who made us.

I write for all those who have a nostalgia for heaven, hardly knowing how to find their way home; for those who are searching for an anchor: the news is that we can get anchored every day to the Source of life.

I write for those who are parched and thirsty in a desert of

[1] John Milton, *Paradise Lost*, Book 3 ll 260–264.

ceaseless activity, who know that there is a river but cannot find their way to it. It is a question of survival; it is a question of desperation. The fact is, there is a well which becomes a stream of inner renewal that can be unblocked.

I write for those who know that something is tugging on their heart calling them to pray. Deep is calling to deep. You have awoken in the night to the sound of your Beloved and you want to let him in! The truth is that all over the world the Spirit of God is awakening people to pray. We are living in the largest world-wide prayer movement ever seen. God is all day long holding out his hands to his people.

I write for all those who are weary and heavily burdened and who long to find rest daily in him. There is a place of rest and quietness to discover.

I write also for those who know that something is up. The Spirit of God is coming upon you with his burden and your life is never going to be the same again.

I write for those who are aware that it is a time as never before to pray; for the intercessors, for those who have their antennae up and who sense that this call to prayer is a work of the Holy Spirit for our generation. There is of course nothing new in the idea that God is looking for a people who pray. Ever since Jesus cleared out the clutter from the temple and declared, 'My house shall be a house of prayer,' we have known the destiny of both the church and our own individual lives. But many are aware of a new intensity, a new hunger, a new parched dissatisfaction with any lifestyle that does not make room for what John the Divine called 'our first love'. Many are also aware of a new energy to pray, but are seeking signposts to go deeper.

I write also for those who hardly know what an intercessor is. You were found by God when you weren't even looking for him. But now that you have glimpsed him, you in turn have to catch hold of his garment and hold on to the One who is the source of life – like the haemorrhaging woman who had waited years for healing and knew instinctively that he is the source of hope.

The twenty-first-century post-modern, post-Christian world is a place of paradox. On the one hand it is a particularly bleak place in which to think and write about prayer. Until recently I have lived and worked in Paris: a particularly fiercely secular environment. Jean-Paul Sartre said, 'I caught the Holy Spirit in the basement of my mind and flung him out of there. Atheism is a long and cruel business. I believe I've been through it to the end. For the last years I've been like a man who no longer has any reason to live.'[2] Many have done as Sartre. Any vestige of Godward impulse they have uprooted in a desire to be bravely modern in a brave new world. But at the same time, the Maker's genetic code cannot be so easily uprooted. They find their hearts restless, for something is missing. Many young people go madly clubbing, raving, keeping awake with Ecstasy or cocaine or tuning in to esoteric religions, but they do not find the life they are nostalgic for as they miss the Source of Life who is called Jesus.

Others continue living wilfully non-religious lives, but find they are shrivelling up daily in an urban desert, 'Living, living and partly living,' as T. S. Eliot put it.[3] Never has the truth of Augustine's words been so achingly relevant: 'Thou hast made us for thyself and our hearts are restless until we find our rest in thee.' Even Bertrand Russell admitted his malaise: 'That God is dead, that I cannot deny. But that my whole being cries out for God: that I can never forget.' This is the paradox that defines the world.

I came across an example of this one Pentecost Sunday. Our church had just finished an open air celebration in a beautiful park/amphitheatre with stunning views of Paris.

---

2 Jean-Paul Sartre, *Words*.

3 T. S. Eliot, *Murder in the Cathedral*.

(For those who are interested, or who may go to Paris, it's a great place to pray for this needy city. Go to the end of the rue Piat from metro Pyrénnées!) As I got talking to a young woman, I asked her why she was crying. 'I don't know.' I suggested it was because she was coming home to her heavenly Father's house. 'But I don't even believe in God. I just came to see a friend.' The more I talked to her there in the park about the love of her Father for her, the more she wept. She didn't become a Christian there and then, but it made me reflect on this paradox.

God is stretching out his hands both to those who are not seeking him, and to Christians who are not in touch with him. The kindness and mercy of God is that, despite our turning away from him, he pours out his Spirit again and again throughout the world. By this I mean that he mercifully visits again and again planet earth with the Spirit of Jesus, as at the day of Pentecost. Many people get caught up in these visitations, which, one could say, are coming with greater intensity and with an accelerated frequency, like the pains of labour. I believe that one particular mark of these visitations at present is that the Spirit of Christ is calling people to be people of prayer. By this I mean people who are in intimate communion with God.

This book is therefore written with the conviction that every Christian is called to pray. And at present the Holy Spirit is calling hundreds of thousands of Christians to be concerned about a deeper prayer life. At the forefront are the intercessors. But is not everyone called to intercede? Paul did not in his letters have a separate section for the intercessors; he asked all the church to pray. Jesus did not call one or two disciples aside to teach them to pray, but he included the whole group. And it was the whole group who pleaded with him, 'Lord, teach us to pray.' E. M. Bounds said, 'Prayer is the easiest and the hardest of all things; the simplest and the sublimest; the weakest and the most powerful; its results lie outside the range of human possibilities . . . Few Christians have anything but a vague idea of the power of prayer; fewer still have any experience of that power. The Church seems almost wholly unaware of the power God puts into her hand. To graduate in the school of prayer is to master the whole course of religious life.'[4] And yet, as I say, the signs are that at last God is waking up his church to pray. It is not the work of man: no man or woman or group could achieve the awakening that we are currently living in. And the purpose of this book is that we should not miss the hour of our visitation.

For many years I have had a kind of motto. I can't remember who I picked it up from, but it was from some Tommy Tenney-style of God-Chaser.[5] It is this: 'My one ambition is this: To find out what the Holy Spirit is doing – and join in.'

There is little doubt that one of the things that the Holy Spirit is doing is pouring out a spirit of prayer in the world. We are witnessing a prayer awakening. On every continent we see the imprint of the Holy Spirit at work. In South America tens of thousands of Christians fill football stadia with the sole purpose of praying through the night. In Goyanya, Brazil, or in Cali, Columbia, Christians are drawn together in unity to seek God, and there are some signs of 'community transformation' as a result.[6] In Africa, we get reports of a million meeting monthly in Nigeria to fast and pray. In Kampala, Uganda, Christians have bought a mountain (literally!) and, under the leadership of John Mulinde, dedicated it to unceasing prayer for revival in every nation of Africa and of the world. In Asia we see on every video of the underground church in China the

---

[4] E. M. Bounds, *A Treasury of Prayer* (Bethany House, 1961) p. 71.

[5] Tommy Tenney, *The God Chasers* (Regal Books, 1998).

[6] See the video *Transformations: A Documentary* published by The Sentinel Group.

tear-stained faces of the intercessors. In North America, what is it that leads a man like Bible teacher Mike Bickle[7] to hand over his church in Kansas City in order to devote himself to leading a prayer ministry twenty-four hours a day, seven days a week, offering unceasing prayer and worship to God?

My answer is that we are living in a particular *kairos*, an alarm clock time when God is waking up his people to pray. Of course this does not mean that we should neglect the other priorities of becoming disciples, understanding and then preaching the kingdom of God and planting churches, but we need to be attentive to the intensity of Jesus' call to be a house of prayer for all nations.

In his excellent book *The Church Is Bigger Than You Think*,[8] statistician and author of *Operation World* Patrick Johnstone notes that 'there is in fact a prayer awakening under way the scope of which would astonish us were we to know the whole story'. He notes five factors: 1. The intensity 2. The militancy 3. The variety of expression, from contemplation to cacophony 4. The global networks of prayer 5. The specific nature of the praying.

How are we to understand this particular time? I believe the prophecy of Zechariah 12:10 is helpful to our understanding this: 'And I will pour out on the house of David and the inhabitants of Jerusalem a spirit of grace and supplication.' There is a spirit of prayer (supplication), and the grace, i.e. the energy, the enabling, the easy yoke with which to fulfil it. Often the marks of this prayer are an intensity, a weeping, pleading, all-together-in-one-place crying out to God, reminiscent of Acts 2 and 4 and Joel 2. Catholic theologian Peter

---

[7] Author of *Passion for Jesus* (Kingsway, 1994) and *Growing in the Prophetic* (Kingsway, 1995).

[8] Patrick Johnstone, *The Church Is Bigger Than You Think* (Christian Focus, 1998).

Hocken interprets 2 Corinthians 5, which speaks of the Christian 'groaning inwardly', as referring to intercession.[9] The intercessor in this move of God is often someone who is so longing to see the coming of the kingdom of God that he is gripped with prayer like the pains of childbirth, often accompanied by 'groans that words cannot express'. Fasting is another aspect of this 'grace' that is being given. In my experience, when the spirit of grace and supplication is poured out, fasting which was before a pain becomes a privilege. It becomes a sweet, wooing call coming from the heart of the Father. And the intercessor is glad to 'hunger for God' rather than for food. Really!

And in Europe I have been amazed to see the level of prayer rising. In France, where I had the privilege of working for nine years, we saw an unprecedented move of prayer.

I am gripped by at least ten different reasons to be passionate about the 'discipline of intimacy' with God.

1. Prayer is our home. Deep down we long for intimacy with God because we're made that way.
2. One of the clear works of the Holy Spirit today is precisely to call Christians to a deeper place of prayer.
3. Jesus recommended it.
4. The disciples wanted it.
5. The apostles modelled it.
6. It is the source of holiness. Through prayer sinfulness drops away and Christ's character is formed in us. To pray is to change.
7. Those who pray get in touch with the heart of God and receive his burden.
8. Intimacy with God is the source of power and peace for our lives.

[9] Peter Hocken, *The Glory and the Shame* (Eagle, 1994).

9. God answers prayer, so desperate situations can be brought to him and he will transform them.
10. Finally, nations are transformed through prayer. The destiny of a nation is not in the hands of the politicians or the multinationals but in the hands of the people of God who pray.

Now, the question to ask is: Where does it all begin? How do we catch this healing malady which is a heart full of love for Jesus, and a desire to seek his face and hear his voice above all others? The answer is to discover what I have called 'the discipline of intimacy'. I invite you to turn the pages of this book, and explore different aspects of this priceless treasure. As you do, I hope you will particularly benefit from the reports of different intercessors in the Bible. But above all, I invite you to open your heart and let the sweet call of the Holy Spirit lead you into the presence of Christ.

2

'Remember the Height from which You Have Fallen . . .'

'I found uncommon manifestations granted to me from God. Early in the morning, at noon, at midnight the blessed Jesus visited and refreshed my heart. If the trees of a certain wood near Stonehouse could speak, they would tell what wonderful communion . . . I enjoyed with our blessed God there. Sometimes as I was walking, my soul would make such leaps that it would almost go out of the body. At other times I would be so overpowered by a sense of God's infinite majesty that I would throw myself on the ground and offer my soul to his hands to write on it what he pleased.'

(George Whitefield)[1]

'The Discipline of Intimacy' was suggested to me by a friend[2] as a seminar title. As I explored it, I realised how well it expressed what is needed in so many of our lives today. I was drawn to the famous words of the risen Jesus to the church at Ephesus: 'I know your deeds, your hard work and your perseverance . . . You have persevered and endured

---

[1] *A further account of God's dealings with George Whitefield*, 1756.

[2] My thanks go to Mark Melluish who is the manager of New Wine conferences in England.

hardships for my name, and have not grown weary. Yet I hold this against you: You have forsaken your first love' (Rev 2:2–4). This perfectly expresses the state of so many of us today. We are hard working, and persevering, but the Lord holds out his hands to us and wants us back in our first love.

The parallels between intimate love for God and romantic love between husband and wife are constantly present in the Bible. Solomon speaks of them; Paul refers to Christ's love for the church as being mirrored by a husband's for his wife. And Jesus wants the Ephesians to come back to their first love.

A couple of years ago, my wife Anita and I were doing a marriage seminar in a summer conference and a couple came up to us at the end asking for prayer. The problem was that they had not made love for seven years. I sensed the pain and desolation as we talked about what had led to this. Difficult relationships with teenagers had gradually crowded out all intimacy. The man said, 'My wife goes up to bed and my daughter talks to her in the bedroom for so long I don't feel welcome.' His wife said, 'Yes, but you go to sleep on the couch downstairs and don't come to bed till 2 am. I am just too tired by then!' Had they ever talked to anyone about this? No, never. I asked her if she would like to rediscover intimacy and she replied without hesitation, 'Yes!' Her husband then shot an amazed and hopeful glance her way. I said there was not much time to do more than to pray, and that they needed to talk together more, but I sensed there was hope. Sometimes just the act of bringing a hidden secret, a subject of shame, out in the open is enough to break free from bondage. We prayed for the Lord to give them the desire of their hearts – a restored, intimate marriage.

At the end of the week the same couple came up to us and, with smiles bigger than their faces, began to thank us. I was slightly embarrassed to know what question to ask, but they assured me that they had 'come back to their first love' in every sense of the term!

I believe we can see this story as a parable. Many walk through life longing for intimacy with God but not finding it. They are sleeping through it, or too busy to make way for it. Many sit in our churches week after week without this precious pearl. At the risk of causing some eyebrows to be raised, I want to say that intimacy with God is just as recoverable as intimacy in marriage. It may be difficult to recover, but it is recoverable. And once recovered, it is a joy to maintain, just as intimacy within marriage is a joy to maintain!

Many have had the experience of one or more encounters with God. They may have been dramatic and on the surface, or calm and interior. They may have been noisy or quiet. Any encounter with the living God, however, will have been, inevitably, life-changing. But few have managed to maintain or remain available for a life of intimacy with God. Hence the parched and thirsty look of so many people in churches today. Of course, a mountain-top experience is not for every day. And yet intimacy with God can be a daily experience.

The best example, as ever, is Jesus, who knew the 'mountain-top' experience of the transfiguration, when he was bathed in glory and talked with Moses and Elijah – an event so powerful that Peter, who was with him, never forgot it (see 2 Peter 1:18). Yet Jesus also had the discipline to get up 'very early in the morning to pray' (Mk 1:35). It was this experience of daily communion that, we could say, sustained Jesus.

The Bible tells us of those who lived an exemplary life of disciplined intimacy.

The Psalmists . . . Psalm 1 talks of the promises associated with a life of disciplined meditation – day and night. We are to be like a tree planted by streams of water, yielding fruit.

The Prophet . . . Isaiah who, on his mountain-top, 'saw the Lord, seated on a throne, high and exalted' (Is 6:1), also speaks of being wakened morning by morning with a word, and of the consolation flowing from those who daily talk with the Lord and live in the discipline of intimacy (Is 50:4).

The King . . . Solomon, in Song of Songs 2, speaks of the swooning heart-stopping love affair with God that can be the privilege of those who are intimate with God.

The Apostles . . . Paul, Peter and John all speak of this dimension. Paul talks of being seated with Christ as a matter of daily fact (Ephesians 1). Peter also knew the sustaining and directing voice of God in times such as when he went up on to the roof at midday to pray (Acts 10). And John, on the island of Patmos, seems not to have found it unusual to have been 'in the spirit on the Lord's day' (Rev 1:1).

As with the couple in the story above, who lost intimacy in their marriage, things can happen which cause us to lose intimacy with God. Jesus spoke of the cares of this world which grow up to choke the good seed. So the cares of work, the stress and pressure of earning a living in a merciless economic climate, can rob us of intimacy with God. Bereavement, loss, shame, unemployment, disappointed hopes, broken relationships can all choke our life hidden with God in Christ. Change, moving house, marriage, work, the arrival of children can all take over our lives to such an extent that our walk with God is put on the back burner and dries up. This section is written to address the question: how can we come back to this first love? How can we rediscover intimacy with God? Or how can we discover it if we have never experienced it?

The words of the risen Christ are very helpful here: 'To the angel of the church in Ephesus write: These are the words of him who holds the seven stars in his right hand and walks among the seven golden lampstands: I know your deeds, your hard work and your perseverance. I know that you cannot tolerate wicked men, that you have tested those who claim to be apostles but are not, and have found them false.

You have persevered and have endured hardships for my name, and have not grown weary. Yet I hold this against you: You have forsaken your first love. Remember the height from which you have fallen! Repent and do the things you did at first' (Rev 2:1–5).

In this passage there is a threefold process. First, they are to remember the height from which they have fallen; second, they are to repent; and third, they are to do the things they did at first.

The discipline of remembering

This is a good exercise and is often recommended in the Bible. Many of the old covenant instructions were given with this in mind. The first chapters of Deuteronomy are all about steps to take 'lest your children forget' the great acts of deliverance of God from slavery. And one of Jesus' great signs, left for us today, is that of the bread and wine that we are to eat and drink 'in remembrance'. What then is it that Revelation wants us to remember? What is the 'height from which we have fallen'? If we remember that the passage is speaking to the church at Ephesus, we can believe the key is in the stories of the birth of the church in Ephesus. These are found in Acts 19, which speaks of twelve disciples who listened to Paul: '"John's baptism was a baptism of repentance. He told the people to believe in the one coming after him, that is, Jesus." On hearing this, they were baptised into the name of the Lord Jesus. When Paul placed his hands on them, the Holy Spirit came on them, and they spoke in tongues and prophesied' (Acts 19:4,5).

To complete the picture in Ephesus, Paul is later involved in arguing the cause of the gospel in the lecture hall of Tyrannus (a kind of prototype Alpha course). There are dramatic scenes of healing and deliverance, people leaving occult practices and burning their costly books, as well as persecution and accusation. A final key to understanding the meaning of the 'height from which they have fallen' is Paul's teaching to the same Ephesians in his letter to them. 'God, who is rich in mercy, made us alive with Christ even when we were dead in transgressions – it is by grace you have been saved. And God raised us up with Christ and seated us with him in the heavenly realms in Christ Jesus' (Eph 2:4).

All of this shows us that for the Ephesians to remember the height from which they had fallen was to remember something that was an event, an experience and a theological fact. The first step, then, to coming back to our first love and to intimacy with God is to remember our conversion. Until the age of twenty-four I was not a Christian. I became convinced about Jesus through my girlfriend's insistence that I read the Bible with an open mind. As I did so, I was deeply drawn to Christ; I felt his magnetic pull. I argued vainly with my girlfriend (who later became my wife), and wrote letters refuting the arguments in books like *Mere Christianity*, which I had been lent. But I knew that the Bible rang true, and as soon as I understood the arguments about the evidence for the resurrection, I began to see they were convincing. I wondered why I was so reluctant to become a Christian, and realised that I was intellectually prejudiced against believing. I had studied French enlightenment literature and the existentialists at Oxford University, and all my training told me that to believe was to commit intellectual suicide! I began to go to church occasionally to see if the church matched up to what I was reading about. Then one Sunday morning I heard a strong call to conversion from the pulpit of a church in Oxford, and, in a prayer with a pastor after the service, surrendered to Christ. The effects were not immediate, but the next morning when I woke up it was as if someone had turned on the lights. It was as if the world up to then had been black and white, and now was suddenly filled with colour. I began to devour the Bible, reading whole tracts of it at one gulp. This is my height to remember.

The Ephesians might have remembered their experience of baptism in water, or how as hands were laid on them they spoke in tongues and prophesied for the first time. They may have remembered burning their occult books, or being healed or delivered from oppression. Do you have an experience of these things? I remember clearly the time I first experienced the fullness of the Holy Spirit, then speaking to God in a new language and prophesying. I had become thirsty for a more biblical experience of a relationship with God. I longed to pray and hear his voice. Some months after my conversion, I began actively seeking him. To cut a long story short, I found myself at a large gathering of Christians where this passage of Acts 19 was being preached and prayer was being offered for those who wanted to 'receive the Spirit' or who wanted the Spirit to 'come on them' as upon the Ephesians. The speaker prayed for me and I was taken up into the presence of God. I remember going away alone into a field afterwards and just sitting for an hour gazing on the beauty of Christ and speaking to my Father in the new language that was pouring out of me. This unblocked a period of intimacy with the Father through Christ which was my period of 'first love'. I began to understand the things Paul speaks about in Ephesians 1 and 2. There he says that we are blessed in the heavenly realms with every spiritual blessing in Christ. He says that God chose us in him before the creation of the world to be holy and blameless in his sight.

He says that God has made known to us the mystery of his will. He says that we have been marked in him with a seal, the promised Holy Spirit, who is a deposit guaranteeing our inheritance until the redemption of those who are God's possession – to the praise of his glory.

Paul is praying that we will have the eyes of our hearts enlightened, that we may know the hope to which he has called us, the riches of his glorious inheritance in the saints, and his incomparably great power for us who believe. That power is like the working of his mighty strength, which he exerted in Christ when he raised him from the dead and seated him at his right hand in the heavenly realms, far above all rule and authority, power and dominion, and every title that can be given, not only in the present age but also in the one to come.

He also says that God, even when we were dead in our transgressions and sins, made us alive with Christ. By grace we have been saved and raised up with him and seated in the heavenly realms in Christ Jesus.

These mysteries become clear to us as God pours his love into our hearts and shows us Jesus and his magnificent loving work of reconciling us to the Father.

I want to ask, do you know and experience this today? Or have you abandoned your first love? If you have abandoned this, then take time to do the first 'spiritual discipline' – remember! Remember the height from which you have fallen. Take time now to remember.

For those who have nothing to remember

Perhaps you really do not have such an experience to look back on, when, having discovered Christ, the Holy Spirit spoke to your spirit and said that you are a child of God. If so, my advice is to ask for it in prayer. You could say something like this:

Lord Jesus, I am thirsty to know God. I am hungry for the bread of life. I want to know you. I am so sorry for the years when I forgot about you. I have gone away from your ways like a lost sheep. I am so sorry. I want to come back to you, the Good Shepherd. Thank you that you died on the cross instead of me. Now please come and take up residence in all the rooms of my life. Come in as my Lord and as my

Shepherd. Lead me to the water of life. Fill me with your Spirit. I love you. Please fill me with your love. Amen.

Remember the height

It is wise to pause for a moment to reflect on this expression 'the height', or the words of Paul that we are 'seated with Christ in the heavenly realms'. It seems that it is part of the inheritance of the Christian to be able to come into the presence of the Father. This is in a way the whole subject of this book, that this is the daily inheritance of every believer. And once we are in the glorious presence of the Father, then we will pray. Later on, we will look at different intercessors and compare notes with them, as it were. But for now, let us make a distinction between the next emotional quick fix, and settling into the peace and joyful embrace of our 'first love'. How quickly, instead of remembering, we forget.

T. S. Eliot caught this in his poem 'Little Gidding', where he evidently refers to the call of Christ:

With the drawing of this Love and the voice of this
Calling
We shall not cease from exploration
And the end of all our exploring
Will be to arrive where we started
And know the place for the first time . . .
A condition of complete simplicity
(Costing not less than everything)
And all shall be well and
All manner of thing shall be well . . .[3]

'Remember the height from which you have fallen.' As we look at different intercessors, we will see that they are each

[3] T. S. Eliot from 'Little Gidding', *Four Quartets* (Faber & Faber).

in the heights with God. We will see Abraham holding on and pleading for Sodom and Gomorrah; Moses asking God to 'show me your glory'. Of Moses it has been said: 'Intimate though he was with God, his intimacy did not abate the necessity of prayer. This intimacy only brought clearer insight into the nature and necessity of prayer, and led him to see the greater obligations to pray, and to discover the larger results of praying.'[4] We will consider the secret history of Hannah, desperately pleading out of barrenness, holding on as it were to the hem of Christ's garment before breaking through to fruitfulness. We will look at the brokenness of Joel, calling a whole nation back into the presence of the living God; at Jeremiah's gift of tears, so frequently found today; or Isaiah, who called for watchmen to join him on the heights of the walls and to give themselves no rest. We will look at Paul's discipline of intimacy, he who knew about the height so much that he was 'caught up to the third heaven' and heard 'inexpressible things, things that man is not permitted to tell' (2 Cor 12:1–3). We will learn from the Master Jesus, whose great longing was that his house should be a house of – what? Cell groups? Seeker-sensitiveness? Community and social action? Cool post-modern awareness? No! Just a house of prayer. A house of prayer for all nations. A place where all humanity can come into or come back to a love affair with God.

---

[4] E. M. Bounds, *A Treasury of Prayer* (Bethany House, 1961), p. 24.

3
The Discipline of Repentance

'Before we set out on the so-called thrilling adventure of prayer, it cannot be too strongly stated that nothing more significant, more awe-inspiring, can occur than meeting the God we set out to meet. It is essential to realise that we will lose our life in the process: the old Adam we are must surely die.'

(Metropolitan Anthony)[1]

'When I start to remember his floods of tears I myself begin to weep, for it is almost impossible to pass dry-eyed through the ocean of his tears. There was never a day or night . . . when his vigilant eyes did not appear bathed in tears.'

(Gregory of Nyssa)[2]

'If I could play all the memories in the neck of my guitar
I'd write a song called . . . a necklace of tears
And every tear a sin I'd committed oh these many years
That's who I was; that's the way it's always been.'

(Paul Simon)[3]

---

1 Metropolitan Anthony, *Living Prayer* (DLT, 1966).
2 Gregory of Nyssa, speaking of St Ephrem, quoted by Richard Foster, *Prayer* (Hodder & Stoughton, 1992) p. 37.
3 Paul Simon, 'You're the one' (Warner Bros, 2000).

The second piece of advice given to those who have abandoned their first love is to practise the discipline of repentance. Repentance involves essentially change. It is not nearly as popular as the other 'R' words today – revival, renewal, restoration – but it is perhaps more biblical and more essential. It is a change of heart and a change of action. It may involve tears. It may be the work of a moment or it may take time. If it is a deep move of God in our lives, it is good not to be in a hurry over it.

The gift of tears

I remember a young teenage girl in Brazil coming forward after a meeting and weeping for many minutes. She was inconsolable. When we asked her what was going on she said, 'My father is not a Christian, but tonight I can believe he will become one. I am weeping out of gratitude, but also out of regret that I have not prayed for him more, and talked to him more. I am resolving to change.'

Sometimes tears will come as we regret our neglect of intimacy with God. You can feel this regret under the surface in Song of Songs 5: 'I slept but my heart was awake. Listen! my lover is knocking . . . I have taken off my robe – must I put it on again? I have washed my feet, must I soil them again? . . . I arose to open for my lover, and my hands dripped with myrrh, my fingers with flowing myrrh, on the handles of the lock. I opened for my lover, but my lover had left; he was gone. My heart had gone out to him when he spoke. I looked for him, but did not find him. I called him but he did not answer.'

Many Bible passages speak of grief and tears in prayer. One such is Zechariah 12:10: 'And I will pour out on the house of David and the inhabitants of Jerusalem a spirit of grace and supplication. They will look on me, the one they have pierced, and they will mourn for him as one mourns for an only child, and grieve bitterly for him, as one grieves for a firstborn son.'

As the spirit of prayer is poured out, the tears of regret flow. This is a precious gift that is evident when the Spirit of God is poured out. Often there is a mingling of grief and relief – tears of relief that there is hope in God and tears of grief that we have neglected him.

For those who cannot cry

Often we meet those who say that they can't cry because of their upbringing. Jeremiah expresses this: 'O that my head were a spring of water and my eyes a fountain of tears! I would weep day and night for the slain of my people' (Jer 9:1). Being around those who can cry may help us to get in touch with the burden of the Holy Spirit. Perhaps this is why Jeremiah says later: 'Call for the wailing women to come; send for the most skilful of them. Let them come quickly and wail over us till our eyes overflow with tears and water streams from our eyelids' (v. 17).

During the past years, I have often seen men overcome with grief and howl in the place of prayer. It is not that we need to become maudlin and emotional. But as deep calls to deep and as the Spirit of God falls, we may find this mixture of repentance and intercession coming upon us with tears.

Many of us will find ourselves blocked off from this precious gift of tears because of past pain in our lives. I myself stopped crying at the age of fourteen when, out of the blue, my parents got divorced. I dried up emotionally almost overnight. I resolved from then on to be brave and to protect myself against any further pain. But inside I was bleeding. It wasn't until ten years later, at the time of being filled with the Holy Spirit, and with the help of my wife, that I dared to express what I was feeling and began to cry again – tears of repentance for the hardness of my heart, and tears of relief because the Holy Spirit was telling my spirit that I was a child of God. They were the tears of another prodigal coming home.

For those of you who feel this is 'just not British', you may well be right. I have been intrigued by Jeremy Paxman's book *The English*. In it he quotes Alan Bennett's definition: 'The English are conceived in irony. We float in it from the womb. It's the amniotic fluid; it is the silver sea . . . the waters at their priest-like task: washing away guilt and purpose and responsibility. Joking but not joking. Caring but not caring. Serious but not serious. It captures one of the essentials of Englishness.'[4]

The French with whom I have worked do not have the same problem. But I don't know if they find tears any easier for all that. Perhaps it is because we are all afraid of emotionalism and are searching for 'real' Christianity. In that case, let me recommend the imitation of Jesus himself of whom it was said, in a seldom quoted text, 'During the days of Jesus' life on earth, he offered up prayers and petitions with loud cries and tears to the one who could save him from death, and he was heard because of his reverent submission' (Heb 5:7). Jesus wept at the tomb of Lazarus and he wept in Gethsemane. But it seems also from this insight into his life that weeping intercession was a part of his daily walk. Let us be imitators of him.

Repentance is not only tears

Repentance is primarily a change of mind and action. When the Ephesians were exhorted to remember and to repent, it was a call to change their forgetful ways and come back to

---

[4] Jeremy Paxman, *The English* (Penguin, 1999) p. 18.

intimacy. In Acts 19, repentance involved the burning of books on the occult. In our church in Paris, I knew this to be necessary for some, as a sign of hating sin and desiring radical change. For some of us the problem may be an idolatry of wealth – a materialism which deadens us and keeps us running with no time for God. We have a life which is the very opposite to that of living by faith. We need to repent. For others it may be bitterness, unforgiveness or anger which haunts us and which we need to confess. For others, repentance may involve the giving up of books or videos or magazines filled with pornography, or the giving up of habits of television watching that wash our minds with images that rob us of our first love for God. This is one example of spiritual adultery that often needs radical action today. I remember a young man coming forward for prayer once who was looking to be filled with the Holy Spirit. But he had a problem which he wanted to confess: addiction to pornography. His marriage six months earlier had not helped him to break free from something he was ashamed of. He had never talked to anyone about the problem, but as he brought it out into the open, and as we prayed, God answered and the bondage was broken and he became free. The results were that he was filled to overflowing with the love of God and rediscovered his 'first love'.

The same is true of television addiction. It can wash our brains of any hunger for God. The small screen is getting larger, and if we are stuck glued to it every night till late, our capacity to get up with energy to seek God in the morning will be dulled. The thing needful is to repent. For both these things, it may be good to ask for help. If you are married, agree together to limit television watching and help each other (gently!) to repent. You may find that accountability and asking for prayer from others can break the cycle. Other events can rob us of intimacy with God. I remember talking with a newly married couple who had completely interrupted their hitherto effective prayer life when they got married. The lack of privacy and time, and the different rhythm of life had blown apart their 'discipline of intimacy'. They needed to talk and resolve to change.

E. M. Bounds says: 'Let us thoroughly understand ourselves and understand this great business of prayer. Our one great business is prayer and we will never do it well without arranging the best conditions of doing it well. Satan has suffered so much by good praying that all his wily, shrewd and ensnaring devices will be used to cripple its performances.'[5] We need to repent of getting ensnared and break free.

Often, in addition, pain, loss and bereavement can threaten our fruitfulness like the winter frost can kill a plant not well rooted. Some twenty years ago our family went through a tragedy that still affects our lives today. Our first, beautiful, apparently perfect son died in his sleep without any explanation. It was cot death, something that I had hardly heard of at the time, although within days I had become an expert on the subject. My wife and children and I entered a period of colourless existence in a desert where there was little spiritual water; a desert in which Anita showed her incredible strength and deep love and trust for God. For myself, I went through the motions. I was a pastor, preaching about the love of God, but wondering why he had not answered my prayer and healed my son as I'd held the limp body in my arms in that cold hospital and called out to him. I knew without a shadow of a doubt about the hope of the resurrection; I knew that the 'promise was for me and my children' (Acts 2:39). But my wife and I missed our son terribly.

Then three years later, when I least expected it, I was 'surprised by joy'. I was assisting at a conference on the

---

[5] E. M. Bounds, *A Treasury of Prayer* (Bethany House, 1961), p. 25

kingdom of God. The coffee break came and the preacher came over to me and prayed for me. Suddenly it was as if heaven opened. I felt the weight of the glory of God come down on me and pretty soon I couldn't stand up, but was lying along one of the pews, laughing and crying at the same time. The preacher moved off, to be replaced by one of his team, who asked me what I thought was going on. I said I felt that the strong hand of God was on me and I was aware, physically, of his love. I felt he was speaking to me about this event. I still didn't understand what had happened to my son,[6] but I knew that God the Father loved me. It was as if his cloak of glory was upon me, and I could hear his voice telling me, 'Charlie, my son, I love you. You don't have to strive. You don't have to prove anything. I am for you. You are my son in whom I am well pleased.' I was crying and laughing at the same time, tears of grief and of relief. I got up from that encounter a new person. It was a time of profound repentance. It was the mercy and love of God that had wooed me to repentance, but repentance there surely was, and there was a deep change. Whereas for the past three years I could hardly listen to a sermon about healing without feeling physically sick, now, although I still did not understand why my son had not been healed in the sense I and Anita had prayed for so desperately, I knew afresh that Jesus is the Healer, for he had healed me! I was keen to pray for the healing and comfort of others with the comfort I myself had received from God (2 Cor 1:3). And as for intimacy with God, I couldn't wait to get alone with him, and come back to the love I'd had at the beginning.

Some reading this chapter may be in a dark night of the

---

[6] We received many letters trying to help us understand at the time. But there are events that even as Christians we should not feel we have to try to explain.

soul. You are perhaps in the middle of the 'evil day'. Well, hang on and look forward to the deliverance of God, when the winter ends and the spring comes again, and he gives you a time of sweet repentance.

4

'Do the Things You Did at First'

'There must be time for Him, just to love Him and have Him love us, no other agendas, no lists of prayer requests. These may come later, but we need to put loving Him first, because only as we are filled with His love, do we have love to give away. So many Christians cannot rest in His presence but must constantly be on duty . . . Our highest calling is to intimacy with the living God. I do not want to hear the words, "Depart from me I never knew you". I want the love affair to grow.'

(Carol Arnott)[1]

'There seems to be a new quickening. The worship in the church becomes warmer, something comes back which had gone, a warmth and a tenderness. There is an encouragement. There is a new wistfulness, a new sense of expectation, a new freedom in the prayers of the people. That is the return of the cloudy pillar. We must be on the alert to discern this . . . Less of the hardness and glibness, and a new tenderness, a new concern, a

---

1 Carol Arnott, *The Purpose of Soaking in His Love* (Spread the Fire, Summer 2001).

new note of agony. Some old people I remember used to say that the thing they were looking for was the element of "Oh", the longing, the groaning, the waiting, the "Oh". And when that comes back it is a sign that the cloudy pillar has come back.'

(Martyn Lloyd-Jones)[2]

All over the world, God is calling his people back to their first love. When we come back to the sweet presence of God and back to our first love, we may feel it is a contradiction in terms to 'do the things we did at first'. We don't want to do things, we want intimacy. But this is to misunderstand the nature of these things. We want to consider in this chapter the things that lead to intimacy.

Steps to intimacy

1. Make a rendezvous first thing each day

Just as in a marriage great gain can be had when the couple have a date night regularly, so with the Lord of heaven it is good to keep a regular time or times with him. The difference is that he seems to prefer the morning! Perhaps this is because it is then that we are preparing for the day ahead of us. As they say, the band doesn't tune up after the performance. Find a special place and choose a special time. Just as in a marriage it is not only good to communicate and listen well every day, but also good to go away alone for special times of marriage renewal, so special days of retreat can significantly renew our walk with God. As regards the daily discipline, many agree that there is nothing better than early in the morning, before the concerns and rush of the day have come upon us. The psalmist says, 'Early will I seek you'; Isaiah talks of being 'woken morning by morning' with a

---

[2] Martyn Lloyd-Jones, *Revival* (Marshall Pickering, 1986) p. 171.

word. And Jesus was up 'very early in the morning' to pray. So, if you want to do the things you did at first, it is probable that they will include time with him early. For some of us this will require drastic action. I remember David Watson telling us that once, when living in community, he was so keen to seek God early that he bought two alarm clocks. One he set for 6 am in his room. The other he put in the corridor outside set at 6.10 am. If he failed to get up with the first alarm, the whole household would know that he had overslept again!

2. Remember how to climb into the presence of God

Through the blood of Christ, we have access into the presence of the Father. This is the heart of the matter. It is good to remember your first love, and how you knew the presence of God around you and upon you. For some it is through worship: if so, put on some worship music. For some it is through confession of sin, although for others this will come later. For some, it is through 'soaking' in the glory of God. For some it is a gradual progression as in Psalm 95: declaring the deeds of God, then declaring who he is – a shepherd – and who we are – the sheep of his pasture. Then it is that we humble ourselves and bow down. Physical posture is important for some, irrelevant for others. I find it helpful to stand with my hands uplifted at times, or to be stretched out on my face (taking care not to fall asleep!). Psalm 95 says the same: 'O come let us worship him and bow down and kneel…' Physical positioning to match a spiritual truth.

3. Learn to love God

It is such a privilege to draw near to God and to love him. The door for communion stands ajar, but it is rare to find people who enter into the holy place daily. Too busy, too tired, too bent by care, we need to straighten up and worship. 'We are here to be worshippers first and workers only second . . . The work done by a worshipper will have eternity in it.' This old dictum of Tozer[3] is still true today. Sometimes this 'embrace' is well expressed by the saints of old. For example Thérèse de Lisieux said this of her love for Jesus: 'I was at the most dangerous time of life for young girls, but God did for me what Ezekiel recounts: Passing by me, Jesus saw that I was ripe for love. He plighted his troth to me and I became His. He threw his cloak about me, washed me with water and anointed me with oil, clothed me with fine linen and silk and decked me with bracelets and priceless gems. He fed me on wheat and honey and oil and I had matchless beauty and He made me a queen. Jesus did all that for me. Jesus did all that for me.'[4]

She speaks, as do others like her, in terms of almost disturbing intimacy. Yet if we are called first of all to love God with all our heart, we should not be surprised if we are drawn to expressing this love in similar terms. I encourage you to try. For example, why not try writing a love song to Jesus? Here is a great example from Tim Hughes:

Day after day I'll search to find you,
Day after day I'll wait for you.
The deeper I go the more I love your name.

So keep my heart pure
And my ways true
As I follow you.
Keep me humble;
I'll stay mindful
Of your mercies, Lord.

I'll cherish your word, I'll seek your presence,
I'll chase after you with all I have,
As one day I know I'll see you face to face.[5]

---

[3] A.W. Tozer, *The Pursuit of God* (Christian Publications, 1982).
[4] Thérèse de Lisieux, *Autobiography* (Doubleday, 1957) p. 62.
[5] Tim Hughes, 'Here I am to worship' (Thankyou Music, 2001).

And as we stand in the presence of God, then it is that God speaks. To return to Psalm 95: 'Today if you hear his voice, do not harden your hearts.'

4. Learn the discipline of listening to the voice of God

This is important and also mysterious. But our God is a God who speaks. And we may need to tune out other noises to hear him. The Bible says he speaks through nature – the heavens which declare the glory of God; through visions, through a burden that he may give to us. We can and should ask the Holy Spirit to speak to us, particularly to convict us of sin. The Bible speaks of God waking his servants in the night, or speaking to them in shrouded, mysterious ways. We know also that there are times of silence, the silence of God, when the word of the Lord is rare. But the way that God has mostly chosen to speak to us is through his word.

5. Learn the precious art of Bible meditation

My whole life as a Christian has been influenced by Campbell McAlpine, a man whose message was the precious riches to be gained from Bible meditation.[6] What is Bible meditation as opposed to transcendental or yogic meditation? It is eating the words of the Bible and being nourished by them. It is allowing the words of Jesus to feed our souls. Just as a cow chews the grass again and again to extract nourishment, so we can turn a phrase from Scripture over in our hearts until we are fed. We can of course meditate on the context of an incident in the life of Christ; we can imagine the sights, sounds, colours, smells and hear the words as if addressed to us, and since the Christ who spoke them is outside time, they can become his *rhema* or 'now' words to us today. But above all, we are turning over the words of the

[6] See Campbell McAlpine, *Alone With God: A Manual of Biblical Meditation* (Bethany House, 1981).

Bible in our minds and applying them to heal, instruct, fortify and equip our hearts. The psalmist speaks tellingly of this discipline of intimacy: 'Blessed is the man who does not walk in the counsel of the wicked, or stand in the way of sinners or sit in the seat of mockers. But his delight is in the law of the Lord, and on his law he meditates day and night. He is like a tree planted by streams of water, which yields its fruit in season and whose leaf does not wither. Whatever he does prospers' (Ps 1).

Clearly there is a deep love for the law of the Lord, so much so that he is delighted in it. Do you have that experience? He is so delighted that he is meditating day and night. As we come back, remember, repent, we too will find renewed intimacy with God.

In Psalm 119 (a good place to start again for all those wishing to come back to their first love) we read: 'Your statutes are wonderful; therefore I obey them. The entrance of your words gives light; it gives understanding to the simple. I open my mouth and pant, longing for your commands' (vv. 129–131).

We can pray with this psalm: 'Open my eyes that I may see wonderful things in your law' (v. 18).

Or we can add to our meditation the discipline of memorising: 'I have hidden your word in my heart that I might not sin against you' (v. 11).

6. Learn to use a prayer journal

This year my daughter gave me a particularly smart prayer journal for Christmas. It has maps and is leather bound, but otherwise it is just a book with a page for every day. I appreciate her present every day, for it is in this journal that I note down what I feel the Lord is saying to me. Particularly I will note down a short passage of Scripture that I want to meditate on and consider through the day. This has been my discipline ever since I became a Christian. It is not the same as a diary, in that it has to do with intentions and with my walk with God. I encourage the use of a journal because it helps us to summarise our God-ward thoughts. I sometimes write out an intercessory prayer, a bit like writing a letter to God, as I find I can be more clear about the longing of my heart about a subject, and sometimes less sloppy.

Looking back to my journal of twenty years ago, coming out of a time of bereavement, and on my ordination retreat, I wrote the following:

> *3rd July. Praying and fasting in an attempt to meet with the Lord Jesus. What happened was that I was led into a meditation on these words:*
> Jesus, name above all names. *Above all others, you are Lord. You are stronger than presidents and princes, bankers and bishops, you are stronger than the enemy and above death.*
> Beautiful Saviour. *You saved me from a life of aimless emptiness and this year have saved my son from death. You save Annie and me from despair.*
> Glorious Lord. *You are bright and so strong in holiness. We burn in your presence. Our hearts burn in us when we approach you in worship. Glory and honour are your garments. You are Lord and captain of our lives.*
> Emmanuel, God is with us. *I had forgotten that you really are inside me, making your home there. No doubt that's why a song of praise so often wells up to you. The Holy Spirit bubbles over.*
> Blessed Redeemer. *For a lost mankind, you paid the redemption price: your blessed Son. How torn and battered and bitter is the world. And yet God was in Christ reconciling all things to himself.*
> Living Word. *Not only are you alive, but you speak to us as well, and your words bring life to the lost, the broken, the captive – such as me!*

> *After this meditation, as I sought to hear from the 'dear, darling only Son of God, Jesus Christ', he began to speak to me from his word.*[7]

A journal can be an expression of our passionate love for God in the same way that a love letter can be to our beloved.

7. Learn to be equipped for ministry in the day to come

Isaiah speaks of how, as we are listening to the Lord in prayer early in the morning, we will be equipped for the day ahead. This is in a way also the birthplace of prophetic ministry. Isaiah 50:4 says: 'The Sovereign Lord has given me an instructed tongue, to know the word that sustains the weary. He wakens me morning by morning, wakens my ear to listen like one being taught.' As we spend time soaking in the presence of God and meditating on his word, perhaps noting down what he is saying to us, perhaps just enjoying his presence, often he will be showing us 'the word that sustains the weary'. We find that when we meet someone in need later in the day, the word we have been considering will be precisely what is needed to build up and sustain that weary person. Why is it that so many Christians are ineffective and powerless? Surely it is because they are not allowing the word to dwell in them richly each day. Jesus himself illustrates this in the famous incident in Mark 1 when he gets up early in the morning to pray. His disciples come and find him and say, 'Everyone is looking for you!' The reply of Jesus in my opinion flows out of his time with the Father. He says, 'Let us go somewhere else – to the nearby villages – so that I can preach there also. That is why I have come.' Again, he is being led out of intimacy into his day's ministry, with direction and sustenance from God.

---

[7] Words taken from the song by Naida Hearn, © Scripture in Song/Thankyou Music, 1974.

The discipline of a journal helps us in this way as we can look back and remember how the Lord has been leading us. Today I have been encouraged by looking up my notes for New Year's Eve. At the start of this year, I felt the Lord say to me, 'Prepare for the harvest.' I noted down and meditated on the verse: 'Open your eyes and look at the fields! They are ripe for harvest' (Jn 4:35). Partly on the strength of this, we planned a whole week of events for our friends and neighbours in Paris. The results exceeded our dreams: we stumbled, as it were, on a harvest, with people coming to Christ through most unlikely routes. For example, a Muslim woman had a dream in which the Lord was called Jesus. She went to the Mairie (town hall) to find out where to find Jesus, but was told that council workers were not equipped to tell her how to find Jesus. She returned home disappointed but then she had a second dream in which she saw a woman who, she was told, would lead her to Jesus. A couple of days later, she had a knock on the door; there was the woman, a Christian visiting from Africa whom she had never met but recognised from her dream. This woman then brought her to our church. The fields were ripening for harvest, and the Lord was prompting his church to be ready.

8. Learn to pray, learn to become an intercessor

When we 'do the things we did at first', it may be that one of those things is to pray the prayer that Jesus taught us. Someone has said that when the disciples came to Jesus, it was not to ask him to teach them to preach, nor to ask him to teach them to heal the sick, but to *teach them to pray.* It is worth reflecting on why this is: perhaps because it is so difficult, so completely beyond the wit of man, unless he catches it from heaven. Or perhaps it is because they saw that the source of Jesus' power to teach, heal and deliver was in his discipline of intimacy. They glimpsed perhaps that Jesus walked with the Father, communed with the Father, and they were thirsty for the same relationship. The next chapters will examine other intercessors in the Bible and how exactly they entered into the reality of intimacy with God. But before we move on to them, let us pause for a moment with Jesus himself and his precious advice.

9. Learn to speak

Tucked away in Jesus' reply to the request 'Teach us to pray', is the little phrase 'when you pray, say . . .'. It may seem obvious, but prayer needs first of all to be expressed in words. There is a place for contemplation, silence, gazing on the beauty of the Lord. There is silence in heaven – but only, apparently, for half an hour. Many of us don't need to learn to be silent, but to speak. The human being has been so designed that his thoughts often only take form and become coherent as they are spoken or written. Shakespeare understood this when he gave this advice to someone grieving: 'Ne'er keep your hat upon your brow: Give sorrow words!'[8]

Even if the prayer is silent, it is good for it to be uttered, as with Hannah, of whom it was said, while praying for a child, 'Her lips were moving, but no sound was heard.' This is because her prayer was articulate, contentful and specific, as we shall see in Chapter 7. Many who are beginning in prayer and intimacy with God would do well to speak out their hearts, their requests, their praise. The apostle James said, 'You do not have, because you do not ask God' (James 4:2). Often prayer dries up because we do not take the simple step of speaking out loud. It may be a shock to the system to have our tongues untied, but if we will but apply this simple discipline, we will find it bears much fruit.

Some may be hesitant because Jesus' teaching comes after he has apparently warned against too many words: 'But

---

[8] Shakespeare's *Macbeth*. Spoken to MacDuff grieving for the loss of his family.

when you pray, do not be like the hypocrites, for they love to pray standing in the synagogues and on the street corners to be seen by men. Truly, I tell you the truth, they have received their reward in full. When you pray, go into your room, close the door and pray to your Father, who is unseen. Then your Father, who sees what is done in secret, will reward you. And when you pray, do not keep on babbling like pagans, for they think they will be heard because of their many words' (Mt 6: 5–7). The two things the Lord is warning about are first, hypocrisy – praying in public rather than in secret. This is a warning we need to heed today. And second, the danger of 'babbling like pagans', that is to say repetitive mantras which are not heart-to-heart communication. Jesus is not here telling us to be brief and to the point; he is telling us to first have a secret history of prayer just between us and the Father. Second, we are to be sure we mean what we say and are really communicating. We can see he is not against speaking at greater length to God from other statements he makes about prayer, notably when telling the story of the unrighteous judge who judges in favour of the widow who will not be silent. He adds: 'And will not God bring about justice for his chosen ones, who cry out to him day and night? Will he keep putting them off? I tell you, he will see that they get justice, and quickly' (Lk 18:7). Here is a clear instruction to 'cry out to him day and night'. With these things in mind, let us dig deeper into Jesus' answer to the disciples' request: 'Teach us to pray.'

5

The Master Plan of Prayer

'The Lord's prayer is not only a prayer but a whole way of life expressed in a prayer. It is the image of the gradual ascent of the soul from bondage to freedom.'

(Metropolitan Anthony)[1]

'For sheer power and majesty, no prayer can equal the Paternoster . . . It is really a total prayer. Its concerns embrace the whole world, from the coming of the kingdom to daily bread. It is lifted up to God in every conceivable setting. It rises from the altars of the great cathedrals and from obscure shanties in unknown places. It is spoken by both children and kings. It is prayed at weddings and death-beds alike. The rich and poor, the intelligent and the illiterate, the simple and the wise – all speak this prayer. As I prayed it this morning, I was joining with the voices of millions around the world who pray in this way every day. It is such a complete prayer that it seems to reach all people at all times and on all places.'

(Richard Foster)[2]

---

[1] Metropolitan Anthony, *Living Prayer*, pp. 27–54.
[2] Richard Foster, *Prayer* (Hodder & Stoughton, 1992) p. 195.

For the past fifteen years, it has been my discipline to pray this prayer nearly every day as a set of jumping-off points for deeper prayer. In my experience nothing is so complete, profound, all-embracing as this discipline of intimacy, as taught by Jesus. Sometimes in the watches of the night when sleep has fled away, it has been balm to my soul. Often in conferences I have led churches and groups through this progression of intercession. It is seldom possible to get through in under an hour. So, if you are looking to pray longer and deeper, why look any further? I first learnt this discipline from John Wimber, who was a father to so many of us and whom we still so deeply miss. He taught something that is not new but which is profound, namely to use each phrase as a springboard for meditation-inspired intercession.

Our Father

Begin your prayer by worshipping the Father and thanking him for the miracle of adoption and free access to his loving presence. In a way this is the key to all Christian prayer – to call God Father. For those whose earthly father has been absent or dangerous or lost in some way (even though he may have been physically there), it may be hard to trust God as Father. If a visible father has turned away from you, how hard to trust an invisible one! Only the Holy Spirit telling your spirit that you are a child of God can lead you to pray 'Our Father, my Father' and mean it, but the Holy Spirit is a specialist in this area, and when you get this, in a way you've got everything – healing, purpose, hope, family identity, joy and peace in believing! It is like a new birth; indeed it is what Jesus called 'birth from above'. This is why it is good not to hurry over this simple phrase, but to take time to get seated in the heavenly places as a child and if a child then as an heir! For this time, try singing worship songs or listening to some anointed, Father-directed worship. Enjoy the heights of the Father's embrace.

And begin ministering to him. When my children were small, I would come back through the door at the end of the day to be greeted by the sweet cries of 'Daddy, Daddy, Daddy!' as they ran at me with their little arms outstretched for me to pick them up into my arms. Even if the fingers they rubbed in my hair were full of banana pulp, I didn't mind! They were healing my day's care out of me. So too with our heavenly Father, who delights to see his children's arms stretched up to him as they call him Father.

In heaven

Recently I was speaking on this subject to a group and was intrigued to find people coming up to me in the break to tell me about visions of heaven that they were repeatedly having at the time: Intimations of Immortality. Have you ever meditated on this fascinating subject? Jesus has gone to prepare a place for us and perhaps this is why he includes heaven twice in the prayer. It helps us to be focused, not on the things of earth but on our treasure in heaven. It is a good thing for Christians to meditate on heaven. There is a place where sorrow and sighing have gone. When the time comes, we can look forward to a place where he will wipe away every tear from our eyes, and death shall be no more, neither shall there be mourning nor crying nor pain any more, for the former things have passed away, and all is righteous. For those who have a son, a daughter, a father or a mother, a husband or a wife in heaven, it is a sweet comfort to pray to the Father in heaven each day and to know that one day we will be there, through the suffering of Christ. Let us rejoice in this. E. M. Bounds said towards the end of his life, 'The best of all is God with us . . . When He is ready, I am ready. I long to taste the joys of the heavenlies.'[3]

---

[3] E. M. Bounds, *A Treasury of Prayer* (Bethany House, 1961), p. 20.

There will be a river there, the river of the water of life, bright as crystal, flowing from the throne of God and of the Lamb through the middle of the street of the city. Also, on either side of the river, is the tree of life with its twelve kinds of fruit, yielding its fruit each month; and the leaves of the tree are for the healing of the nations.

As we look up to the Father and 'climb into his presence' through Christ, we can be deeply refreshed by 'the river', as many today call the renewing, soaking work of the Holy Spirit. And as we stay in the river we may, like John, see heaven opened and glimpse what John glimpsed. The throne of God and of the Lamb shall be in it, and his servants shall worship him; they shall see his face, and his name shall be on their foreheads.

This prayer to God in heaven leads us inevitably forward to later sections in Jesus' prayer and the soon coming of the King: 'The angel said to me, "These words are trustworthy and true. The Lord, the God of the spirits of the prophets, sent his angel to show his servants the things that must soon take place." "Behold, I am coming soon!"' (Rev 22:6–7).

There will inevitably be a mingling of worship and intercession when we think of God as our Father in heaven. Let us pause for a moment to consider Martin Luther, who said that he had so much business he could not get on without spending three hours a day in prayer. One of his fellow ministers gives this report: 'Once I happened to hear him at prayer. Gracious God! What spirit and what faith is there in his expressions! He petitions God with as much reverence as if he were in the divine presence, and yet with as firm a hope and confidence as he would address a father or a friend. "I know", said he "thou art our Father and our God; and therefore I am sure that thou wilt bring to nought the persecutors of thy children. For shouldest thou fail to do this, thine own cause, being connected with ours, would be endangered. It is entirely thine own concern." While I was listening to Luther pray in this manner, at a distance, my soul seemed on fire within me.'[4]

So, intimacy leads to intercession. But before that, and still in this context of intimacy and worship as we begin to pray, Jesus teaches us to think on his name.

Hallowed be your name

It is interesting that Moses, who perhaps had had more encounters with the living God than anyone, was still, even after Mount Sinai, hungering to know more of the glory. Exactly who was this God he had encountered in the wilderness and who had led them out of Egypt with a mighty hand?

Moses had three prayers that we would do well to emulate today: 1. Teach me your ways. 2. Let your presence go with us. 3. Show me your glory. When he prayed this last prayer, the Lord replied, 'I will cause all my goodness to pass in front of you, and will proclaim my name, the Lord, in your presence' (Ex 33:19). When Moses hid himself in the rock, and the glory of God and the name of God were revealed, this is what happened: 'Then the Lord came down in the cloud and stood there with him and proclaimed his name, the Lord. And he passed in front of Moses, proclaiming, "The Lord, the Lord, the compassionate and gracious God, slow to anger, abounding in love and faithfulness, maintaining love to thousands, and forgiving wickedness, rebellion and sin. Yet he does not leave the guilty unpunished; he punishes the children and their children for the sin of the fathers, to the third and the fourth generation." And Moses bowed to the ground at once and worshipped' (Ex 34:5–8).

We learn from this passage the close link between the glory, the name and the character of God. The glory of God is his character: slow to anger, just, forgiving, righteous,

---

[4] *Ibid.* p. 70.

eternal. And his character is his name. Hence when Jesus calls us to hallow the name of God, he is calling us to meditate on his character. And, like Moses, we will be drawn to worship as we sense the presence of the glory of God.

I encourage you not to hurry over this phase of the discipline of intimacy. American prophetic teacher Ruth Heflin liked to say: 'Praise Him till the spirit of worship comes; Worship Him till the glory comes; then Stand in the Glory of God.'[5] This is one way to 'hallow his name'.

This perfect phrase of Jesus' prayer expresses this aspect of the knowable yet unknowable God. We can think of the names of God in the Old Testament and memorise them and the incidents to which they refer. This will be an edifying, faith-building time each day as we 'practise the presence of God'. It is so good to proclaim him as Jehovah Jireh: 'Hitherto the Lord has provided'. To remember also that he is a shepherd who guides and leads is a good thing, and it will keep us flowing out in worship to him. Here are some more of the precious names of God in the Old Testament that can fuel our prayer:

Jehovah Tsebaaoth	The Lord of Hosts	1 Samuel 17:45
Jehovah Elyon	God most high	Psalm 7:18
Jehovah Jireh	God my provider	Genesis 22:14
Jehovah Roï	The Lord my shepherd	Psalm 23:1
Jehovah Nissi	The Lord my banner	Exodus 17:15
Jehovah Shalom	The Lord my peace	Judges 6:24
Jehovah Shammah	The Lord who is there	Ezekiel 48:35
Jehovah Tsidkenou	The Lord our righteousness	Jeremiah 23:6
Jehovah Mekadesh	The Lord who sanctifies	Leviticus 20:8
Jehovah Raphé	The Lord who heals	Exodus 15:26

[5] Ruth Heflin, *Glory* (McDougal Publishing, 1996).

Elohim	God in plurality (three persons)	Genesis 1:1
El-Elohé Israël	The Lord the God of Israel	Genesis 33:20
Adonaï	My Lord	Genesis 15:2
El Shaddaï	All-powerful Lord	Genesis 17:1
El Olam	Eternal Lord	Genesis 21:33
El Gibbor	Strong God (Champion)	Isaiah 9:5
El Elyon	Most high God	Genesis 14:18

We will also find ourselves drawn to the names of Christ both in the Old and New Testaments: Emmanuel, Wonderful Counsellor, Everlasting Father, Prince of Peace. We can repent for the scorn in which his name is held, as well as proclaim him out loud as the Light of the world, the Gate to heaven, the Resurrection and the Life, the Way and the Truth, the Bread of life, the Baptiser in the Holy Spirit and with fire, the Alpha and the Omega. We can think of him as the one who rides a white horse, whose name is Faithful and True, whose eyes are a blaze of fire. We can proclaim that the name by which he is called is the Word of God. We can call to mind that 'on his robe and on his thigh he has this name written: King of kings and Lord of lords' (Rev 19:16). These are just some of the names that we are to hallow. As we do so, we may be led in prophetic proclamation over our city, declaring that there will come a day when his name will be hallowed, and when every knee will bow and every tongue will confess that Jesus Christ is Lord (another of his names!). This brings us to the next phrase of the prayer.

Your kingdom come, your will be done on earth as it is in heaven

Th'infernal serpent . . . him the Almighty Power
Hurled headlong flaming from th'ethereal sky
With hideous ruin and combustion down

To bottomless perdition, there to dwell
In adamantine chains and penal fire,
Who durst defy th'Omnipotent to arms.[6]

John Milton in writing *Paradise Lost* certainly understood the meaning of the power of the kingdom of God, way above all other powers on earth or in hell. When we pray for the coming of the kingdom we begin to touch and enter the realm of spiritual warfare. Ask now for the leading of his spirit as regards what aspects of his kingdom and his will to pray about. It is a vast subject, the coming of the kingdom of God, and we move from worship to intercession with this phrase. The kingdom of God is the rule of God, the inbreaking of his reign on earth that is so complete in heaven. The kingdom of God has to do with the conversion of the lost, the healing of the sick, the deliverance of the oppressed. It comes as the body of Christ on earth advances, so it has to do with church planting and church growth, the equipping of the saints for the work of ministry. The coming of the kingdom speaks also of a concern for the nations to hear the gospel and to be reached for Christ, perhaps especially in difficult areas such as the 10/40 window[7] where faith in Christ costs the most.

In this section, we may be led to pray for the government and those in authority, as Timothy was instructed (1 Tim 2:1–2), and to pray for righteous decisions and laws. We may be burdened concerning giant issues such as globalisation, ecology, slavery, poverty. Or these things may be beyond us, we 'do not concern ourselves with great matters' and we want in prayer just to 'quieten our soul like a weaned child

---

[6] Milton, *Paradise Lost*, Book 1 ll 44–49.

[7] The 10/40 window is a missiological term for the 'window of land' between latitudes 10 and 40 which contains the least evangelised and the poorest countries in the world.

with its mother' (Ps 131). How we need to have the mind of the Holy Spirit to lead us! Paul says that we do not know how to pray but the Holy Spirit intercedes for us with groans too deep for words (Rom 8:26). In a sense the rest of this book is a meditation on this, looking at how the intercessors of the Bible went about the business of praying for the kingdom of God.

But in the daily discipline of intimacy, I want to add that it is good to be focused. This is why some Christians like to keep certain subjects in their prayers day after day, week after week. My friend Phillippe Joret, a devoted intercessor for France and the French-speaking world, is so disciplined that he knows that each day he will be covering different parts of his many concerns in intercession. Others are less left-brained and more spontaneous. For myself, I have periods of each. At present in my prayer journal, I have maps of the different continents before me most days to remind me to pray for friends labouring there, or key works of God that need prayer. I believe a combination of disciplined praying through certain subjects, balanced with Spirit-led spontaneity, is what is needed as we pray for the coming kingdom.

And give us today our daily bread

In countries of extreme poverty, of course, this text takes on an acutely poignant ring. Families all over the world are looking up to God by faith and praying this prayer, particularly for their malnourished children. We can pause to pray and listen to the Holy Spirit as we consider this.

It is typical of the down-to-earth friendship of the Son of God for man that he, knowing our preoccupations, should swiftly move from wide concerns of the kingdom to those of the home and the need for food. In the West, we can be comforted that those who have financial difficulties can bring them to God in this prayer. This is the mystery of the love of God. Those who are threatened by debt or unemployment can call out for help. Those whose families are struggling are encouraged to pray for material release. It is not a prayer for prosperity, but a prayer for the richly symbolic 'bread'. Those who carry the needs of their church community before God can pray for the provision of work for the unemployed. Since moving to an area of higher unemployment these last years, I have been amazed to see the effectiveness of praying for work for those who have none. Even this month, we saw a man who had lost his job in unjust circumstances and who was at risk of bankruptcy, extraordinarily find another within days and be back in the position to buy his daily bread.

'As every day demands its bread, so every day demands its prayer . . . Today's manna is what we need.'[8] The prayer also reminds us of the truly extraordinary story of daily manna in the wilderness, which God provided with the aim that his people should learn to trust him. As I write this section there are those in my church threatened with redundancy. It is a stressful, potentially anxious time. Nothing is certain. Nothing, that is, except the fact that, in this trying time, they have an opportunity to pray 'Give us today our daily bread' and an opportunity to trust him.

Bread has a rich meaning in the Bible, and it is right also to extend our prayer for daily bread to the realm of spiritual bread from the One who is the Bread of life. I am praying in this section for my wife and children to be feeding on the word of God. I am praying for them to read the Bible daily and for it to build them up, just like food. I am praying for them to have a close walk with God and to know how to hear his voice; to feed on and be nourished by the word of God and not by other foods that will never satisfy. I am praying

---

[8] E.M. Bounds, *op cit*, p. 124.

the same thing for my brothers and sisters and parents, that they too would not starve for want of real bread. As someone who is 'carrying a burden' for a church, and to a certain extent a nation, I am wanting my church to be fed. I am praying for the preaching of the word in our church to be true, effective and nourishing.

This prayer is an interesting prayer to pray in seasons of fasting. John Wesley said, 'The man who never fasts is no more in the way to heaven than the man who never prays.'[9] It is hard to overstate the importance of this spiritual discipline. Many Christians are being graciously wooed back to it, myself included. We will return to this theme in Chapter 8, but suffice it to say here that as we fast, we are not doing it to exert pressure on God, but to say, 'I am hungry above all for you! To know you and to feed on you.' So it is that we may find ourselves fasting and still saying 'Give us today our daily bread.' As John Piper says, 'Fasting is the physical expression of our heart-hunger for the coming of Jesus. Fasting poses the question: How much do we miss him? How hungry are we for him to come?'[10]

And forgive us our sins

The psalmist said: 'If I had cherished sin in my heart, the Lord would not have listened' (Ps 66:18). As we are in this dynamic of prayer, there will already have been confession of sin as we worshipped in the first stages of the prayer. But it is wholesome for there also to be a time when we ask the Holy Spirit to come and show us any area of our life which is not pleasing to God. It is a good idea consciously to ask the Holy Spirit to speak to us, and not to feel that we already know our sin. The heart is so deceitful. Perhaps there have

---

[9] Quoted in John Piper, *A Hunger for God* (IVP, 1997) p. 191.
[10] *Ibid.* pp. 83, 84.

been wrong attitudes, things said that were unloving, or things left unsaid that withheld love or appreciation. As we ask the Lord Jesus what he thinks of us, he will no doubt tell us, if we really want to know! Werner, a close friend and one of the pastors of our church in Paris, is a man who is very sensitive to the Holy Spirit. If he feels he has grieved him he will not rest till he has put things right. He has sometimes rung me from another country to ask forgiveness for a word out of season. Even if I may not have noticed there was a problem, I value his zeal not to grieve the Holy Spirit.

This can be a time also to bring to God any 'besetting sins' or areas of defeat that you wrestle with. Although one can argue that there should be no such thing in the life of the Christian, there may be a period of struggle for release in an area. I have known people to struggle over financial difficulty for a period of years before finding the years of jubilee and freedom from debt finally arrive! In the meantime, they are pleading the cross of Christ, praying for forgiveness and release, until it comes.

Quite recently, during a retreat, I met a 70-year-old woman who asked for prayer. She was apparently radiant and a loving full-time church worker (though officially retired). When we got talking, it transpired she doubted she was a Christian at all because of an inner vow to Satan she had taken when only seven years old. She had tried to forget and had succeeded for most of the time. But now she found herself more and more conscious of her bondage. I asked her if she had ever told anyone about it and she said no, not even her husband who had recently gone to be with the Lord. I asked her if she had at some point given her life to Christ and she replied that she knew she had clearly done so. As she began to renounce this vow, she suddenly broke out in a weirdly different voice: 'You don't think you're going to win, do you?' I replied that Jesus had already won and that the time had come for the evil spirit to leave her.

This it then clearly did, cleanly, if a little noisily. The result was joy unspeakable all over the dear lady's face, a joy which lasted. Up till then, she had been praying 'Forgive me my sins' daily. God is just to forgive us and to cleanse us from all unrighteousness, as the epistle of John says, but there are times when we can only stand confessing our sin before God over a period of time until deliverance comes. But come it will.

This prayer for forgiveness can also extend to confessing the sin of a nation, otherwise known as identificational repentance. We will return to a fuller treatment of this theme in Chapter 8. This is what Nehemiah did when he heard the news of the broken down walls of Jerusalem and of the ruin of the city (Nehemiah 1). He broke down, wept, fasted, prayed and said, 'Let your ear be attentive and your eyes open to hear the prayer your servant is praying before you day and night for your servants, the people of Israel. I confess the sins we Israelites, including myself and my father's house, have committed against you.'

In our times of prayer daily, it is good to be asking for the forgiveness of God for our nation. It is part of the discipline of intimacy too. There come particular times when we feel the hand of God preparing to visit a nation or a continent, and many voices are saying that now is the time for Europe. If this is the case, any visitation from God is likely to be accompanied by a particular sensitivity on the part of Christians to the state of their nation in the eyes of God, and a desire to ask for mercy.

As we forgive those who sin against us

One of the probing questions of the Welsh revival, which swept 100,000 people into the churches of the principality and changed the face of a nation, was this: 'Have you forgiven everybody, everybody, everybody?' It is a good question to ask of yourself daily too. As we reach this phrase in the prayer, we can ask the Holy Spirit to probe our hearts. Great testimonies are to be found of power released into lives by the fact of actively forgiving and releasing others. Conversely, Jesus says, in his addendum to this prayer, that if we do not forgive, neither will our Father in heaven forgive us. It is evidently a key to life. This is because if we do not release those who have hurt us, and if we imprison them in chains of unforgiveness, then those chains are likely to end up strangling us.

I sometimes think of forgiveness as on a scale of difficulty. At one end there is forgiving those who have failed to talk to us in church and ignored us again. At the other end, and much more difficult, there is abuse in the past, abandonment and real betrayal. Because of the increasingly chaotic life stories in this post-Christian, postmodern society, we find the proportion of those having suffered abuse is rising sharply. In our church in Paris, we were as a result glad to welcome the 'desert streams' ministry, and we had two programmes, one of eight weeks and one of thirty-two weeks, for those in need of healing on a deep level. Often the key moment of healing comes through the decision to forgive.

As we pray 'Forgive us our sins, as we forgive those who have sinned against us', we may be challenged to release those who have hurt us. It is true that without this, the discipline of intimacy will be empty. We can then do what Jesus recommended, namely, we can bless those who have hurt us. Some years ago I came across a parable which expresses this in a graphic way:

> *Some years ago in the town of Füssen there lived an austere baker called Hans. Hans was a God-fearing man who one day came home unexpectedly at midday to find his wife Freda in bed with another man. Freda's adultery soon became the talk of the town. But Hans surprised everybody by forgiving his wife as the Good Book said he should. In his*

heart, however, Hans did not forgive his wife. He hated her more and more every day for betraying him. But Hans' hypocrisy did not sit well in heaven. The legend says that God sent an angel, and every time Hans looked at his wife with hatred, the angel shot a pebble into his heart, and Hans felt a stab of agony. Pretty soon the weight of a stony heart became heavy and Hans could no longer walk upright. He hunched over in pain and he began to wish he was dead. Hans asked if there was any way he might be free, and the angel said that there was one way. He must ask for the miracle of new eyes; eyes that went back to the beginning of his pain, and which saw his wife, not as someone who had betrayed him, but as a lonely woman who had needed his love. At first Hans could not ask, for he had grown to love his pain. But in the end, his agony became too great. He asked, and the angel gave. Not all at once, but gradually, he began to remove the stones one by one. In the end Hans saw his wife in a new, forgiven light. He asked her back into his heart, and they began a second season of love together.[11]

The story is not a condoning of adultery: God forbid! But it does help us to understand what happens when we can't forgive those who repent, and shows the way to begin to do so – by asking for 'God's eyesight'. As we pray, we can actively ask for this. Some years ago I told this story in a church where I was preaching. After the service, Anita and I had a lunch appointment with some people we hardly knew, an apparently successful, happily married couple. We exchanged polite greetings, and during these exchanges I asked them what they had thought of the service. The man hesitated for a moment before saying, 'You know the story you told? Well, I am that man.' His wife began to cry silently as he told us of how she had betrayed him for a time with

[11] Quoted in Lewis Smedes, *Love Within Limits* (Eerdmans, 1978).

another man. 'The difference is,' he said, 'I can't forgive, even though my wife has broken it all off. I still feel terribly betrayed and angry.' Over the next few months we became aware of the devastating effects of adultery and deceit. So I am not saying that such an act is easy. But it will at some point be necessary to avoid the anger killing you.

It is a curious fact that sometimes betrayal in a church context can be almost as devastating. Our reactions often seem out of all proportion. It is only church, after all. This is particularly true of leaders who feel betrayed. Why is this? It is surely because the church, being the body of Christ, is a place where we have let down our masks, given our all, transferred our affections; and this is in a sense not a false or unhealthy transfer. Yet we can and must still forgive, release, bless and not take ourselves too seriously. The prayer of Jesus is there so that every day, if need be (and sometimes it takes days, weeks and even months), we can actively forgive and speak out loud blessing over those who have, we think, betrayed us. There is a teaching in some circles which suggests (following Luke 17:3–4) that we should only forgive those who repent. But we have the fabulous example of Jesus before our eyes, who prayed forgiveness even on those who whipped and spat upon him, because they did not know what they were doing.

And lead us not into the time of trial, but deliver us from the evil one

Strong spiritual warfare against the forces of darkness is something more and more churches are being led into. The fact that this phrase follows the previous one is evidently intentional as one of the main snares of the evil one will be through unforgiveness, which leads to bitterness. Paul said, 'Do not let the sun go down while you are still angry, and do not give the devil a foothold' (Eph 4:26–27). Those who have gone to bed angry days without number may well have need to be delivered from the evil one.

In the West, we may find the question crossing our mind: But does the 'evil one' really exist? It is not the purpose of this book to argue for or justify biblical revelation, so all I will do at this point is quote Martyn Lloyd-Jones' preface to his commentary on Ephesians 6 which, in my opinion, is a sage reply to such thoughts: 'In a world of decaying values, collapsing institutions, increasing anarchy, It is my belief that the present century can only be understood with reference to the particular activity of the 'Prince of the power of the Air; If we cannot discern the chief cause of our ills, how can we hope to cure them?'[12]

In our work in Paris in recent years, Anita and I became more aware of oppressive spirits and the need to confront them. I remember Sandra, who has given me permission to tell her story here. The first time she came to our church in Paris, aged 20, she held tightly on to her mother and was not able to lift her eyes. We learnt that she lived in a locked psychiatric unit for her own safety, as she had tried to take her life by drinking bleach. A childhood story of abuse and shame led her to say to me one day, 'Don't ever talk to me about marriage, Charlie. That will never ever happen to me.'

We decided to have Sandra to live with us and she became like a daughter to us and a sister to our daughters. Yet she still suffered moments of oppression and times of trial, during one of which she again tried to take an overdose. But she was beginning to have her heart warmed by the love of the church for her. Then one memorable night in our church the Spirit of God came in power. Guy Chevreau from Toronto was ministering, but it was during a worship song

---

[12] Martyn Lloyd-Jones, preface to *The Christian Soldier* (Banner of Truth, 1977).

that she fell to the ground and there was delivered from the evil, oppressing spirit that was afflicting her. She joined the music team, and what a joy it was to see her leading the people in worship with her eyes lifted to Jesus. She caught the bouquet at my daughter's wedding a few years later and then last year we had the delight of seeing her walk down the aisle, in the presence of both her parents, having been turned around in her thinking about herself, and 'delivered from the evil one', to get married to Emile! Truly it could be said of Sandra: 'No longer will they call you Deserted, or name your land Desolate. But you will be called [my delight is in her], and your land [married]. For the Lord will take delight in you, and your land will be married' (Is 62:4).

I tell this story to say that the first interpretation of this section of the prayer has to do with deliverance. Secondly, it speaks of protection. Those who have suffered sudden loss or disaster understand what the Bible calls 'the evil day' (RSV). This is the day spoken of by Paul to the Ephesians, when he says, 'Therefore take the whole armour of God, that you may be able to withstand in the evil day, and having done all, to stand.' I remember sitting with Ugandan leader John Mulinde, who lost his 35-year-old wife one evil day in April 2000, leaving seven children and her husband behind her. Speaking about this his reflection was that if the 'evil day' came, and our children were left without us, what are the most precious things we would want to be sure to have bequeathed to them already? But this phrase in the prayer is a prayer for protection against the evil day, that it should not come. What a comfort to be able to pray this. I daily endeavour to lift up a shield around my family and our church that God would protect us and that we would not be led into a time of trial.

I also believe there are times when we may well suffer from the pressure that comes from what the Bible calls 'the accuser'. He is the one who from the pit of hell tries to neutralise us, accuse us, depress us, devour us. According to Paul, we need to resist him. I first learnt to do this in Kampala, Uganda. Perhaps it was that raw atmosphere filled with faith in God, uncluttered by centuries of rationalism, that rubbed off on me. But I began to take authority through prayer, recognising and resisting and fighting against evil, and I have not been the same since.

We can pray the same thing for a nation, and, if God gives you to do this, to wrestle against 'principalities, against the powers, against the world rulers of this present darkness, against the spiritual hosts of wickedness in the heavenly places', as Paul says in Ephesians. How do we do this without overstepping our authority, or without 'babbling like pagans', to use the phrase of Jesus? I believe one key is to pray as Jesus suggests here, asking the Father to keep us safe from trial and to deliver us.

Another key is to be found in submission to the local church and becoming part of the local body of Christ. It is the body of Christ that has the authority to wage this kind of battle against forces of evil over a city or town. The local church will keep our feet on the ground and our head in the clouds! The local church will remind us that in the realm of spiritual warfare, the first place to go about it will be in individual ministry to expel oppressive spirits from individuals. Then there will come a level of authority over spirits in an area, which we are to confront and pray to God for deliverance from. And then over a nation. But the place of safety is the church. It is a good rule of thumb not to pray in private a prayer we would not be at ease praying out loud in our local church. I say this because there are few models for this in the New Testament, and one text, that of Jude verse 9, offers a caution to those who 'pray above their station'. Having said this, Jesus' prayer unavoidably leads us into these realms, and part of the discipline of intimacy is to accept the call to stand clearly in prayer against the enemy. These are things that in years past the apostles to our land understood. Read *St Patrick's Breastplate*, or read the Litany of the 1662 Prayer Book and be encouraged in your authority.

For yours is the kingdom, the power and the glory for ever and ever. Amen.

It is a well known fact that Christ has planned for this time before the presence of God to end caught up in the glory. It is wise that, having prayed and interceded against the evil one, we should give ourselves again to what the Westminster Catechism calls the 'chief end of man', namely worship.

Saying 'Yours is the kingdom, the power and the glory' is to group three current buzz words for charismatics in one phrase. Over the last years in France it was the 'glory' that provoked a rash of books and conferences. As we finish this daily discipline, it is a privilege to reflect on the glory of God, the anointing of God, the cloud of the presence of God, the glorious river that we can come to. We may want to cry out with Moses, 'Lord, show me your glory.' In the Bible, the first time it is a question of glory is when the Israelites are to be delivered from slavery. It is said that through this, the Lord will 'get glory' for himself (Ex 14:4). This is indeed the kingdom and the power and the glory. It is a parable for the nations in which we ourselves are working, a daily reminder that there can be deliverance for them too.

Also, it is the glory that comes down upon the tabernacle and which causes Moses' face to shine. We can be encouraged by the fact that we now with unveiled faces all reflect the Lord's glory, and are being changed from one degree of glory into another. So let's lift up our heads! How will we be changed? Through worship and prayer, through washing our minds with his word, through living accountable lives in communities called churches.

Later on, through the sin of the sons of Eli, it was said of the place of worship and of the people of God, 'Ichabod', the glory has departed. If we are living through a time of weakness, loss or even apostasy in our own church, we can praise God for a day when all things will be made new. 'For yours is the kingdom, the power and the glory.' It was not to be too long before, under Solomon, the cloud of the glory of God was to come down and fill the newly consecrated temple, and the priests could not enter the house of the Lord, because the glory of the Lord filled the Lord's house.

In such a time as this, Isaiah the prophet saw the Lord, high and lifted up, with his train filling the same temple and the angels were crying out, 'Holy, holy, holy. The whole earth is full of his glory.' This may lead us to pray for similar visions of his greatness, that he might open our spiritual eyes to see his angels, or to see his glory on the earth. Like Habakkuk who saw with spiritual eyesight one day that the earth will be filled with the knowledge of the glory of the Lord, as the waters cover the sea, this knowledge of the glory of the Lord is something to meditate over and a reality to have a heart longing for.

In this overview of glory, we have not mentioned the prayer book of the psalms, that rich treasury with its over fifty references to the glory. Nor have we mentioned Jesus. We can discipline ourselves simply to meditate on and hunger to know Christ. For as the writer to the Hebrews says, he is the very image of the glory of God (Heb 1:3). It is fitting to conclude this prayer by simply loving the Lord Jesus. Let us remember that he should be our principal subject of joy. C. H. Spurgeon once went on a European tour and was encouraging his church, if they could afford it, to go and see the Alps: 'Time would utterly fail me to speak of all the wonders of God which we saw in nature and providence.' Then he paused for a moment and added: 'If you cannot travel, remember that our Lord Jesus Christ is more glorious than all else that you could ever see. Get a view of Christ, and you have seen more than mountains and cascades and valleys and seas can ever show you!'[13] This is what we do each time we pray 'For yours is the kingdom, the power and the glory'. John saw this clearly when thinking back on the incarnate Son of God: 'We have seen his glory, the glory of the one and only Son, who came from the Father.' He got a view of the glory as Jesus stunned comprehension at that wonderful wedding when water became wine: 'This, the first of his miraculous signs, Jesus performed at Cana of Galilee. He thus revealed his glory' (Jn 2:11).

The glory of God reaches down into intense suffering. It sees that little daughter of Jairus who was fading out of the world, being sucked by illness down into death, losing touch with her parents who strove to get to Jesus in time, that he might come to her. As Jesus responds, he is delayed on his way by another desperate need, the woman with a haemorrhage. Time stands still. Jairus is told it is too late. Despair comes crashing in. And yet the glory of God is revealed in the healings of both the woman and the child! Jesus, as it were, reaches down his hand into death to pull the little girl back with the precious words, 'Little girl, arise.' This intervention is the glory of God. We know it because of Jesus' later remarks on the illness of his friend, another scene of desperation, when he brings hope to the hopeless with the words: 'This sickness will not end in death. No, it is for God's glory so that God's Son may be glorified through it' (Jn 11:4).

All these incidents are parables for prayer. We will return to them in Chapter 7. But even at this point in our discipline of intimacy, we may be bringing desperate needs for healing before God and 'holding on' for a manifestation of his glory.

In our own church, we were propelled into doing this.

---

[13] C. H. Spurgeon, *Autobiography* (Banner of Truth, 1973) p. 32.

With no warning, after an incident in the delivery room, the tiny daughter of some friends was born with badly damaged lungs, and hung between life and death. The alert came through to the church and we gathered immediately to pray. The Lord gave us tears (which come back to me even as I write this) and urgency and unity to 'hold on to the hem of his garment'. For three full months this little girl was kept in intensive care. Initially she was given oxygen intravenously through her neck, a new process that even the midwives in our church had never heard of. It was deeply touching to see the little scrap of a girl lying sweetly suffering all the tubes without a murmur, so trustingly. Her parents stayed with her constantly, talking with her and praying. They found that many parents stayed away from their children in those wards: from business or pain or a feeling of impotence. But Véronique and Marc stayed and prayed and hung on to God, waiting for his glory to be revealed. Again and again we anointed her with oil, despite the fact that this is a difficult thing to do in a French hospital. Gradually, the breakthroughs began to come. First the parents received what can only be called a gift of faith that their daughter would be restored to them. Then the doctors began to marvel. And sure enough, Lois came home healthy. To see her now never fails to remind me of the glory, the power and the kingdom of God. Véro and Marc hung on in the evil day and, I dare say, saw the glory of God.

Let us draw this extended meditation on how to pray to a close by reflecting that it was clearly Jesus' desire for us to see visions of glory! This was his high priestly prayer in John 17: 'Father, I want those you have given me to be with me where I am, and to see my glory, the glory you have given me because you loved me before the creation of the world' (Jn 17:24). We can be confident that Jesus' prayers can be answered, not only in heaven, but also on earth!

Part 2

ABRAHAM'S STORY

When the men got up to leave, they looked down towards Sodom, and Abraham walked along with them to see them on their way. Then the Lord said, 'Shall I hide from Abraham what I am about to do? Abraham will surely become a great and powerful nation, and all nations on earth will be blessed through him. For I have chosen him, so that he will direct his children and his household after him to keep the way of the Lord by doing what is right and just, so that the Lord will bring about for Abraham what he has promised him.'

Then the Lord said, 'The outcry against Sodom and Gomorrah is so great and their sin so grievous that I will go down and see if what they have done is as bad as the outcry that has reached me. If not, I will know.'

The men turned away and went towards Sodom, but Abraham remained standing before the Lord. Then Abraham approached him and said: 'Will you sweep away the righteous with the wicked? What if there are fifty righteous people in the city? Will you really sweep it away and not spare the place for the sake of the fifty righteous people in it? Far be it from you to do such a thing – to kill the righteous with the wicked, treating the righteous and the wicked alike. Far be it from you! Will not the Judge of all the earth do right?'

The Lord said, 'If I find fifty righteous people in the city of Sodom, I will spare the whole place for their sake.'

Then Abraham spoke up again: 'Now that I have been so bold as to speak to the Lord, though I am nothing but dust and ashes, what if the number of the righteous is five less than fifty? Will you destroy the whole city because of five people?'

'If I find forty-five there,' he said, 'I will not destroy it.'

Once again he spoke to him, 'What if only forty are found there?'

He said, 'For the sake of forty, I will not do it.'

Then he said, 'May the Lord not be angry, but let me speak. What if only thirty can be found there?'

He answered, 'I will not do it if I find thirty there.'

Abraham said, 'Now that I have been so bold as to speak to the Lord, what if only twenty can be found there?'

He said, 'For the sake of twenty, I will not destroy it.'

Then he said, 'May the Lord not be angry, but let me speak just once more. What if only ten can be found there?'

He answered, 'For the sake of ten, I will not destroy it.'

When the Lord had finished speaking with Abraham, he left, and Abraham returned home. (Gen 18:16–33)

6
What Is Intercession?

'Prayer is the Church's banquet . . .
Exalted manna, gladness of the best,
Heaven in the ordinary, man well drest
The Milkie Way, the bird of paradise . . .
The land of spices; something understood.'
(George Herbert)[1]

As we come close to God, two things happen: the first is that we have a revelation of his nature; his character is revealed to us. The second is that he will reveal his plans, or his 'secrets', his projects . . . and his judgements. This is the prophetic nature of intercession. The first will bring us to know God; the second will bring us to know his will. The first will bring us to change ourselves; the second may bring us to be involved in changing history.

These twin aspects of prayer are seen in the experience of Moses. During his first encounter with God, he takes off his shoes: he needs to change to be in the presence of the living God. Then secondly, God reveals his plans: 'I have indeed seen the misery of my people in Egypt . . . So I have come down to rescue them' (Ex 3:7).

[1] George Herbert, *Prayer*.

The first aspect changes us ('to pray is to change'[2]); the second aspect of sensing what the future may be can bring us to a third step: namely, interceding to try to change the will of God! This is true of Moses when the glory of God comes down in a cloud. He has a revelation of God's nature ('holy and to be feared' Ex 19:12). Second, he becomes aware of coming judgement on the very people he leads, because of their stubbornness. Then third, his intercessor's reaction is to plead that God would not act in judgement ('Turn from your fierce anger; relent and do not bring disaster on your people' Ex 32:12).

The prophetic nature of intercession

The prophetic aspect of a prayer life of intimacy with God is dynamically present in the story of the very first intercessor of the Bible, Abraham. The incident in question is the moment when Abraham pleads for the salvation of Sodom and Gomorrah, where his nephew Lot lives.

When we meet him here, Abraham already has a secret history with God. He knows his voice; he has made himself completely available to God. He has travelled all the way from Ur of the Chaldees because of faith in the promises of God. He will be challenged even more poignantly in the future when his long-promised one and only son is asked of him as a sacrifice.

The incident is reported in Genesis 18. It follows the revelation that Abraham and Sarah will have the son they have longed for. Sarah has laughed and then denied it. It is a holy moment. And then this crucial phrase appears: 'Shall I hide from Abraham what I am about to do?' (v. 17). It is almost as if the Lord can't be untrue to his desire for fellowship, trust and to have a people for himself. He will show his hand.

---

[2] Richard Foster, *Prayer* (Hodder & Stoughton, 1992).

He has shown this family that they will have a son and in that son there is a destiny for a people.

Those who pray are almost inevitably aware when 'something is up'. For they are close to heaven, they are close to the counsels of God. Think of Anna and Simeon at the time of the birth of Jesus. Of Simeon it was said, 'It had been revealed to him by the Holy Spirit that he would not die before he had seen the Lord's Christ' (Lk 2:26). Of Anna: 'She gave thanks to God and spoke about the child to all who were looking forward to the redemption of Jerusalem' (v. 38). We think of Moses' remark: 'I wish that all the Lord's people were prophets'(Num 11:29). Or Amos 3:7: 'Surely the Sovereign Lord does nothing without revealing his plan to his servants the prophets.'

It is like a father who has bought a fantastic present for his wife. He can't resist telling the secret to his children, showing them the present and enjoying their excitement (this has happened to me often!). On a more sombre note, when danger is up, or trouble coming, a wise father will gather his family together and warn them as best he can.

This prophetic nature of prayer is part of the privilege of intercession. With privilege, of course, comes responsibility. We are not to fall into fleshly false prophecy. A good safeguard is to be rooted in and accountable to a local church that understands these things, and to become part of an intercession team in the body of Christ.

Finally, this prophetic aspect of prayer will sometimes lead to the biblical fact of the intercessor apparently trying to change the purposes of God.

Let us rejoin Abraham. He is in the presence of God. It is a picture of prayer, of intercession. And in the presence of 'the glory' he has revelation from God as to danger. It has to do with the holiness of God and his hatred of sin.

Here is the Genesis account: '"The outcry against Sodom and Gomorrah is so great and their sin is so grievous that I will go down and see if what they have done is as bad as the outcry that has reached me. If not, I will know." The men turned away and went towards Sodom, but Abraham remained standing before the Lord. Then Abraham approached him and said: "Will you sweep away the righteous with the wicked?"' (Gen 18:21–22).

Abraham reminds me of Hannah, of Moses, of Nehemiah, and in the time of Jesus, of Jairus, of the woman with a haemorrhage; all those who 'held on to God'. Like Jacob, who said, 'I will not let you go unless you bless me' (Gen 32:26). The men go, but Abraham as it were 'holds on to their garment'. This reminds me of the need for the person of prayer to 'stay in the glory of God'; to stay seated in the heavenly places. Do you know this?

In the next moment, Abraham intercedes; he pleads in favour of another that the Lord would intervene. He pleads that if fifty righteous people be found in Sodom, the Lord would relent of his intention to destroy the city. In verse 29 Abraham starts again, and from this we learn about the persistence of the intercessor: 'Once again he spoke to him . . .' Abraham actually negotiates with God the number of 'righteous people' who, if found in the city, would bring a reprieve. He gets it down to ten.

The whole dialogue is fascinating, and is based on the premise that the Lord could change his plan. But can God change his mind? This question is of crucial importance for the one who prays, and it is good to confront it straight on. How we answer this question will have enormous influence on how we pray. Evidently, for Abraham, it was a possibility. This is the famous 'openness of God' theological theory, the supposition that God is susceptible or 'open' in his purposes, and will act according to factors such as the prayer and fervent supplication of the saints, or the repentance of his people. For me it is clear that this is the case, and it is a great incentive to pray.

Another example of the Lord apparently changing his plan is in the story of Jonah and the destruction of Nineveh. Here, the prophetic word that God will destroy the city in three days does not come to pass because of the repentance of the city.

Beyond this, it is fair to say that some see that the prayer and repentance are themselves part of the working of God's will. God's 'otherness' and eternity mean that these things are hard to nail down.

As regards this crucial Old Testament incident with Abraham, we see that with his servant, his friend, his son, the father of the covenant is drawn into relationship and dialogue and that this dialogue takes time. It shows the openness of God to relationship.

Abraham pleads on the basis of God's compassion: 'Will you sweep away the righteous with the wicked?' And because of the just character of God: 'Will not the Judge of all the earth do right?' Also because of his justice: 'Far be it from you to do such a thing.' We can learn invaluable things about the proper basis for intercession from this passage.

In the end ten righteous who are standing together on behalf of their city are not found, and judgement comes. We should be aware of the effect that pride, haughtiness, sin – in this case sexual and homosexual sin, and the sin of taking no account of the poor (see Ezek 16:49) – has on our holy Lord God Almighty.

We should learn to be in relationship with God, to be listening, persistent, coherent. We are to plead on the grounds of God's character, his justice and compassion.

One final thought from this the first of all intercessors and our chief example of a man who walked by faith: Sodom might not have been destroyed had ten men who walked faithfully with God been found in the city. They might have saved their city. And how about our cities today? Does not their sin rise up to God as an offence? And should we not take this incident as a challenge? Let us be those who are in a united communion to plead on behalf of our city that protection might not be removed and that it might not be destroyed.

This lies at the basis of the theology of the 'Transformations' movement. The 'Transformations' video shows how united prayer on behalf of a city like Cali, Columbia, transformed the city from one dominated by the drug barons and under the judgement of violence and murder, to a place of hopefulness – and in a sense avoided destruction. Crime fell and the city began to become inhabitable again.[3] May God help us to 'catch' what the Holy Spirit is saying through the story of Abraham about interceding for our cities today.

---

[3] See also George Otis, *Informed Intercession* (Renew Books, 1999) pp. 37–47.

HANNAH'S STORY

There was a certain man of Ramathaim, a Zuphite from the hill country of Ephraim, whose name was Elkanah son of Jeroham, the son of Elihu, the son of Tohu, the son of Zuph, an Ephraimite. He had two wives; one was called Hannah and the other Peninnah. Peninnah had children, but Hannah had none.

Year after year this man went up from his town to worship and sacrifice to the Lord Almighty at Shiloh, where Hophni and Phinehas, the two sons of Eli, were priests of the Lord. Whenever the day came for Elkanah to sacrifice, he would give portions of the meat to his wife Peninnah and to all her sons and daughters. But to Hannah he gave a double portion because he loved her, and the Lord had closed her womb. And because the Lord had closed her womb, her rival kept provoking her in order to irritate her. This went on year after year. Whenever Hannah went up to the house of the Lord, her rival provoked her until she wept and would not eat. Elkanah her husband would say to her, 'Hannah, why are you weeping? Why don't you eat? Why are you downhearted? Don't I mean more to you than ten sons?'

Once when they had finished eating and drinking in Shiloh, Hannah stood up. Now Eli the priest was sitting on a chair by the doorpost of the Lord's temple. In bitterness of soul Hannah wept much and prayed to the Lord. And she made a vow, saying, 'O Lord Almighty, if you will only look upon your servant's misery and remember me, and not forget your servant but give her a son, then I will give him to the Lord for all the days of his life, and no razor will ever be used on his head.'

As she kept on praying to the Lord, Eli observed her mouth. Hannah was praying in her heart, and her lips were moving but her voice was not heard. Eli thought she was drunk and said to her, 'How long will you keep on getting drunk? Get rid of your wine.'

'Not so, my Lord,' Hannah replied, 'I am a woman who is deeply troubled. I have not been drinking wine or beer; I was pouring out my soul to the Lord. Do not take your servant for a wicked woman; I have been praying here out of my great anguish and grief.'

Eli answered, 'Go in peace, and may the God of Israel grant you what you have asked of him.'

She said, 'May your servant find favour in your eyes.' Then she went her way and ate something, and her face was no longer downcast.

Early the next morning they arose and worshipped before the Lord and then went back to their home at Ramah. Elkanah lay with Hannah his wife, and the Lord remembered her. So in the course of time Hannah conceived and gave birth to a son. She named him Samuel, saying, 'Because I asked the Lord for him.' . . .

After he was weaned, she took the boy with her, young as he was, along with a three-year-old bull, an ephah of flour and a skin of wine, and brought him to the house of the Lord at Shiloh. When they had slaughtered the bull, they brought the boy to Eli, and she said to him, 'As surely as you live, my lord, I am the woman who stood here beside you praying to the Lord. I prayed for this child, and the Lord has granted me what I asked of him. So now I give him to the Lord. For his whole life he shall be given over to the Lord.' And he worshipped the Lord there. (1 Sam 1–20, 24–28)

7
Desperate Prayer

'Desire has a tremendous motivating power in prevailing prayer; the deeper your desire to see God's answers, the deeper your hunger to see God at work . . . the more powerfully the Holy Spirit can pray through you. Holy desire is a holy power that energises prayer.'

(Wesley Duewel)[1]

'He who desires not from the depths of his heart makes a deceptive prayer.'

(François Fénelon)[2]

The story of Hannah told in the first chapter of 1 Samuel is one that has fascinated me in these last few years. I believe that in it we have a key for understanding how to turn desperate situations of sterility into opportunities to see the answers of God. If we learn the lessons of praying for our own areas of sterility, and break through in these areas, we will understand how to pray for our nations, who are gripped by the paralysing sterility of unbelief.

---

1 Wesley Duewel, *Mighty Prevailing Prayer* (Zondervan, 1990) p. 67.

2 François Fénelon, quoted in Arthur Mathews, *Born for Battle* (STL, 1978) p. 115.

When we pick up this story, we see that Hannah is sterile and broken and has been for several years. Her situation speaks of the desperate grief of childlessness. Some are given special grace to face this, but others who long for a child but cannot have one know the monthly, searing despair that flows over a whole marriage. The story can also speak about other forms of 'sterility'. For some, singleness is, after a time, like a curse. Again, some are called to singleness, which can be an honourable condition leading to great fruitfulness. Others, however, long for a husband or a wife. They don't feel at all 'called' to stay single. They are desperate, just like Hannah was desperate. For some, the sterility may be financial: debt haunts them and defeats them, and however they try, they can't break free to victory. This can be one of the most debilitating things for a marriage or for a family, causing deep conflict and even separation. For others, sterility means their children being off the rails or unconverted. Whatever they do, things don't change, year after year. For others work is a drudge – or unavailable. Others are dogged by illness, like the woman with an issue of blood for many years. They know they need to hold on to the hem of Christ's garment, and yet they can't seem to get to him.

Hannah is despised and ridiculed and provoked year after year by her rival. But instead of getting into a clinical depression, she reacts by choosing the most powerful weapon that exists: she prays. Indeed it is more than the destiny of the nation that will literally be in the hands of one sterile woman. For in the end, Hannah will give birth to Samuel, and Samuel will pull the whole nation of Israel back from idolatry. Hannah's son will anoint kings. And it is from one of them, from David's line, that a child will eventually be born who is to be the Saviour of the world.

So it is that we can say that the destiny of a nation is not in the hands of the politicians or the business people but in the hands of the people of God who pray. When we realise this we will strain our eyes to look closer to see exactly what are the elements of Hannah's intercession. Can she too 'teach us to pray'?

First of all, we see that she refuses the status quo. Her husband asks her the reasonable question: 'Don't I mean more to you than ten sons?' Hannah politely replies: 'No.' Elkanah is trying to comfort her, trying to make peace, trying to lead her to a place of maturity and acceptance. But Hannah will not accept it – even after years of barrenness. Whether it is childlessness or singleness, financial strangulation or a lost family, a barren work situation or unemployment, or the trauma of illness, maybe it is time not to accept the status quo and to pray desperate prayers like Hannah.

As a pastor, I know how delicate a question this is. If we take the example of terminal illness: there does come a time when we need to put our house in order and accept that we are going to die. Great harm can come from living in denial, and failing to prepare with one's family and before God for the end. But for many that time is not yet. They need to stand up and fight the status quo as Hannah did.

Second, we see she is fasting (verse 8). This is a precious, gracious, wooing call from heaven. Fasting is on the menu of the church worldwide today as never before. We will look at this in more detail in the next chapter.

Third, there are tears in her eyes. Verse 10 says, 'In bitterness of soul Hannah wept much.' Again it's a gift poured out in the world today, which we looked at in Chapter 3. I like the verse from Psalm 56:8: 'Gather my tears in your bottle, are they not all written in your book?' (AV). Some people find they cry so much in prayer that they wonder what is wrong with them. Well, I want to say you're in good company. Jesus himself wept in prayer and he said that those who mourn are blessed – perhaps because they are the ones who are expressing their need of God, and he will not despise their broken and contrite spirit. Often we feel we should pull ourselves together and cheer up. But sometimes to do so will be to let go of God. Instead, learn to get in touch with the desires of your heart, and pour them out before God.

I remember a life-changing conversation with my wife, Anita. She pleaded with me early on in our marriage to dare to express what was going on deep down. It was something I had never learnt how to do before, but she said, 'I don't hold out much hope for our marriage if you won't tell me what you are feeling.' In the same way, we are the Bride of Christ, and he wants us to entrust him with our depths, which at times will involve tears.

The fourth element of Hannah's prayer life is that there is a history of abandonment. Like Abraham, a progression is described here in Hannah's relationship with the Father. That is to say, it is almost as if the answer is withheld as Hannah changes, and her motives come into line with those of the Lord. Can God withhold a gift to test our motives, even the gift of a child? Well, God is God; he can do as he likes. And the apostle James says, 'When you ask, you do not receive, because you ask with wrong motives, that you may spend what you get on your pleasures' (Jas 4:3). But now Hannah has arrived at a place of true abandonment: 'She made a vow, saying, "O Lord Almighty, if you will only look upon your servant's misery and remember me, and not forget your servant but give her a son, then I will give him to the Lord for all the days of his life."' This is the passage often quoted at baby dedications. But it is far more than just a baby dedication, it is a giving away to God of the answer to prayer itself! Think what this means: when the longed for baby son arrives, almost at once Hannah will give him up and let him go out of her house. Those who have sighed as their children leave home after their teenage years sometimes feel pain. Hannah lets him go almost as soon as he has come! She will give up the fruit of her own prayer.

One commentator put it like this:

'If Hannah's prayer for a son had been answered at the time she set for herself, the nation might never have known the mighty man of God it found in Samuel. Hannah wanted a son, but God wanted more. He wanted a prophet, and a saviour, and a ruler for His people. Someone has said that "God had to get a woman before He could get a man." This woman He got in Hannah precisely by delaying the answer to her prayer, for out of the discipline of those weeks and months and years there came a woman with a vision like God's, with tempered soul and gentle spirit and a seasoned will prepared to be the kind of mother for the kind of man God knew the nation needed.'[3]

This also is a mysterious element of intercession. It comes from something done and seen in secret. It is a kind of covenant in private with God. I think this is the kind of thing Jesus was thinking of when he said, 'When you pray, go into your room, close the door and pray to your Father, who is unseen. Then your Father, who sees what is done in secret, will reward you' (Mt 6:6).

A secret history with God

This fifth element often comes hand in hand with abandonment. Hannah's covenant with God is part of her 'secret history'. Do you have a secret history that only you and God share? I have an example of this in my own life from the time when I heard the call of God to go to and work in France.

Although I was drawn to France, serving the church there was something I was reluctant to do, as France has the reputation of being 'the graveyard of missionaries'. In fact it is hard for British Christians to imagine the poverty of

---

[3] W. E. Biederwolf in E. M. Bounds, *A Treasury of Prayer* (Bethany House, 1961), p. 176.

the evangelical church in France. Centuries of humanistic philosophical tradition have taken their toll. Together with this, France saw fierce persecution of Protestants in the sixteenth and seventeenth centuries, and then a bloody revolution at the time when England was seeing revival. And since then France has become a proudly secular society. All this has made church planting in France no easy task.

Yet I sensed the call of God, and the very first time I went to France to explore this call, I was more or less offered a job – to pastor the tiny Eglise Réformée de Belleville in inner-city Paris. The time came when I went to Belleville to 'preach with a view'. When I got there my whole being rebelled against the prospect. I found the place dirty, polluted and forbidding. I could not imagine squeezing my family into the apartment that went with the job. In fact, the first time we showed the apartment to our children, we had to climb over a prostrate body blocking the entrance, and my daughter whispered, 'Is he dead?' I saw from the empty bottle lying beside him that he was not dead, but sleeping.

The multi-cultural community intimidated me. Belleville contains Algerians, Turks, Chinese, Vietnamese, Greeks, French West Africans, Europeans, Muslims, Jews and Hindus. It is as if you change country every ten yards as you walk down the rue de Belleville. I could not imagine building a church there, let alone trying to do so in a foreign language. That evening I did an open air event with a Youth With A Mission team in the red-light district of Pigale. It was one of those events where no one stopped to talk. The passers-by exhibited the most supreme indifference to our efforts.

By the time I got to bed that night, I was in trouble. 'O God, get me out of here!' I prayed. I was intimidated, and the last thing I wanted to do was to move from green and pleas-

---

[4] 'Better a soft soft pillow for that old gray head, than the churlish turf of France.' (Shakespeare: *Henry V*).

ant church-rich England to 'the churlish turf of France'.[4] However, I summoned up enough faith to pray a secret prayer to my Father in heaven. I knew from past secret-history prayer times (on the day before my application to the pastoral ministry thirteen years earlier, for example) that God had promised me that I would bear fruit. I argued with God that I couldn't bear fruit in France. In the end I prayed a prayer like this: 'O God, if you want me to come here with my family, and to bear fruit in your kingdom, please show me in this way: when I preach tomorrow, let one person at least be converted to you. Then I will know and I promise I will go. My life belongs to you.'

I thought this was a pretty safe bet, given that only thirty or so people, apparently, would be in the service the next day, and it was to be my first ever sermon in French. The day dawned and I preached on Matthew 21 about the cleansing of the temple. I talked about God wanting to cleanse his church and fill it with his presence. And I added that he also wanted to come and cleanse individual temples, individual lives. Anyone who wished to invite Christ to clear out the rubbish from their life and take up residence as their Lord, I would be happy to pray with at the end. As the service finished, a curious thing happened. I sensed the deep love of God for that local church and a few minutes later a young student came up to me. As we got talking, he told me that he had been wondering about Christianity and becoming a Christian for some time and that he was ready to make the decision – which he then did as we prayed together. I didn't know whether to laugh or cry. 'Oh no! God has answered my prayer!' was about my reaction.

The effect of this was that my life swung around as if on a hinge and from then on I knew. It was not as if I did not have doubts or fears; in fact, I am ashamed to say I had many, and even put the move off for a year or two. But I knew that I knew that I knew that God had called me. This in turn gave me what I would call a platform of authority, so that when in France I began to call people to conversion, I knew they would come. When I wrote out a vision statement with the elders for the future growth of the church, I knew that there would be growth, because I knew that God had called me in secret. So it was that the forty present on our first Sunday soon became eighty, the eighty became 150, the 150 became 300, the 300 grew slowly but surely to be 400, and the local church, in difficult soil, grew and continues to grow.

The first Sunday that we were there after our move to France, a young doctor joined the church. One Sunday, nine years later, after the second morning service, she looked out over the church. 'You know, Charlie, even if things are sometimes difficult, one thing I'm sure of is this: the Lord really does love this church.' I agreed with her. I looked at the multitude of nationalities living together (we counted thirty-four nations on one Pentecost Sunday service alone). I looked at the young mingling with the old. I remembered the kindness of God, in one moment of secret prayer with him, to include me in his love affair with his church in every nation.

What are the reasons for the growth we saw? One may be the changing climate in France. André Malraux has famously said: '*Le 21ème siècle sera religieux ou il ne sera pas.*' ('Either the twenty-first century will be spiritual or there won't be a twenty-first century.') And there is a growing hunger in France for God.

Another reason may be the prayers prayed in secret for revival in Belleville over the years, including mine. Hannah knew this love from God for the people of God, and she knew it in a moment of abandonment, a moment of secret, personal covenant with God.

The sixth thing we see from the account of Hannah's desperate dealings with God is that she was filled with the Spirit as she prayed. The account says that 'Hannah was praying in her heart, and her lips were moving, but her voice was not heard. Eli thought she was drunk' (v. 13). The passage makes me think of the day of Pentecost and the gift of the Spirit that made the passers-by believe the disciples were drunk. Some might add that perhaps Hannah was speaking in tongues. We will return for a discussion of this vital gift for the intercessor in Chapter 10. For the moment what I would like to underline is that she was burdened by the Holy Spirit. Paul says, 'The Spirit helps us in our weakness. We do not know what we ought to pray, but the Spirit himself intercedes for us with groans that words cannot express' (Rom 8:26). This is a vital key for anointed intercession: we must have the Holy Spirit. Prayer without the anointing and leading of the Spirit will be a work of the flesh, a dead work, and a tiring one at that. Prayer yoked up to the Spirit of Jesus will have an ease and fluency and enabling about it even though the burden and the effort and energy may be considerable.

E. M. Bounds said: 'We pray not by the truth the Holy Spirit reveals to us, but we pray by the actual presence of the Holy Spirit. He puts the desire in our hearts; kindles the desire by His own flame. We simply give lip and voice and heart to His unutterable groanings.'[5] We will look more closely at this and the phenomenon of 'birthing prayer' when we consider the apostle Paul in Chapter 10.

Seventh, Hannah is misunderstood and criticised by her leaders. Eli accuses her of being drunk, and effectively tells her to pull herself together. Those who follow hard after God will suffer misunderstanding and criticism. Those who become addicted to prayer may also be criticised. Those who welcome the anointing and groaning burden of the Holy Spirit may well be ridiculed. This was certainly the case for me in the years I worked in the French Reformed Church,

---

[5] *Op cit*, p. 56.

a denomination which rejected the use of charismatic gifts since the time following some excesses during the persecution of the Huguenots, and because of the writings on the subject of that famous Frenchman, John Calvin.[6] Sartre's remark quoted earlier could also apply to this denomination: 'I caught the Holy Spirit in the basement and flung him out of there,' although there are notable exceptions to this. When a wave of renewal hit us in 1994, we were as an eldership summoned before regional councils and the like. We were accused, not of being drunk, but of having people fall down in trances, which of course is worse!

What shall we say of this? First, it is important not to seek to imitate outlandish behaviour which is of no value. Second, we should not be surprised if we are criticised as the Holy Spirit comes upon us. It is not inevitable, but it is possible that it will happen, especially in the historic denominations. Third, we need to emulate Hannah, who had 'the gentle answer [which] turns away wrath' (Prov 15:1). When accused she did not take offence at Eli's lack of discernment. She did not slam the door and change churches! What she did was to explain carefully to Eli what was happening.

We see this in a similar incident in the life of Peter in Acts 10. He is awakened by the Holy Spirit to an unheard of activity, namely to go and visit a non-Jewish community with the gospel. He is sharply criticised for this. He then takes trouble carefully to explain his actions and the fruit of them. He is then understood and fellowship is restored with the Jerusalem church. In our own situation, we found the same thing happened. We carefully explained why this or that

---

[6] Calvin taught that the gift of tongues for worship had ceased. See for example his commentary on Acts 10:46: 'Therefore God took away that shortly after which he had given and did not suffer the same to be corrupted with longer abuse.' *Calvin's Commentaries*, Vol XVIII (Baker Books edn, 1979) p. 453.

action had happened and the result was a cautious welcome. The Proverbs verse in full says: A gentle answer turns away wrath, but a harsh word stirs up anger. Let the intercessor be someone who does all he can to avoid stirring up anger. Exactly the same thing happened to Hannah. Here is her careful explanation: 'Not so, my lord, I am a woman who is deeply troubled. I have not been drinking wine or beer; I was pouring out my soul to the Lord. Do not take your servant for a wicked woman; I have been praying here out of my great anguish and grief.'

As a result of this (eighth) Hannah receives the blessing of Eli. She receives the promise – from God and from Eli – by faith. This also is important for the intercessor. There comes a time where the burden lifts, and it is possible to rest in the provision of God. Not to do so would be a sin. It would be as when a child, whose parents finally promise to grant a request, nevertheless keeps on asking about it, not believing them. Let us as intercessors learn to recognise the moment of a request granted.

The ninth aspect of Hannah's journey is that she co-operates in the natural realm to bring about what has been promised in the spiritual realm. Effectively this means that she and Elkanah make love. This is how the Bible puts it: 'Early the next morning they arose and worshipped before the Lord and they went back to their home at Ramah. Elkanah lay with Hannah his wife, and the Lord remembered her.' We must always remember the relationship between prayer and action. Each without the other becomes a dead work. God is a God who works in the natural realm. So those interceding passionately for an end to their unemployment must also take a rendez-vous at the job centre. Those longing to get married must look outward and be open to the friendships God may open up and be ready to be beautified. I remember one young man in our church talking to me about his desire to get married. He had had a difficult background and for a period of his life had lived rough on the streets, and you could still sense this in his appearance even though he now had a job and an apartment. I said gently, 'Well, if that's the case you need to burn those clothes and buy some new ones.' He did, and two years later I had the privilege of presiding at his wedding.

Finally, and joyfully, in this story 'the Lord remembers her'. It is not that he has forgotten her, but rather that he now brings into being the promises of his covenant agreement. Hannah gives birth to Samuel who, lent to the Lord as he is, makes way for the salvation of Israel, the coming of the king, and, indirectly, the coming of the Lord Jesus.

In our situations of barrenness we can go through these ten stages of prayer with Hannah. Refusing the status quo, fasting, weeping, abandonment, having a secret history, being filled with the Spirit, being misunderstood but with a 'soft answer that turns away wrath', receiving the promise by faith, co-operating in the natural realm and, finally, the almost unutterable joy of the Lord 'remembering' her.

Postscript

This story of Hannah invaded our own family in Paris in an unforgettable way. At a certain period, one of our children was going through a rough time, as only teenagers can. She has given me permission to tell her story. It is difficult enough to be a Christian teenager amidst the pressures of a godless society, but to be one in a foreign culture where it is hard to make close friends with your peers because of lack of language fluency is a tall order. One of our children had found it particularly difficult to survive and, unknown to us, had taken to skipping school and drifting through Paris, partly because of a sense of inadequacy at school and at home. One day she simply disappeared, and when the school contacted us, we came face to face with the reality that had been largely hidden from us. That day Anita and I did not react as mighty people of faith but as parents who felt terrified for their child. Anyone who has known, even for a moment, the disappearance of a child will identify with the crashing panic that invaded our lives that day. We experienced fear that we hardly knew existed, and we did not cope well.

I telephoned the elders of our church to say that I would not be coming to the elders' meeting that night and explained the situation. I said I needed to stay with my family. I asked them to pray. This was the first time I had ever missed a meeting, so they knew something serious was up.

We spent the evening imagining the worst. I telephoned every contact I could think of for my daughter, but drew a complete blank. After a while someone came to the door. It was the Ugandan leader, John Mulinde. By coincidence he was in Paris for a week visiting our church and had been delegated to come and pray with us by the elders whom he had been due to address that night. We explained the situation to John, whom we hardly knew at the time. He had been in Uganda under the dictatorships of Idi Amin and then Milton Obote, and had lived through the disappearance of children. He knew what it was for a child or a loved one not to come home. He said to us, 'Well, in a situation like this, all we can do is pray.' With Enos, his collaborator, he then knelt down in our sitting room and began to pray.

It is hard to describe what happened next. My three other children were there with us, and we all knelt down and all, I think, began to cry as John prayed with us. We were not having a prayer meeting, we were praying. We were not even praying, we were pouring out our hearts before the Lord. Anita, my children and I were burdened by concern, but also burdened by the Holy Spirit. Tears were falling freely, we were holding on to the Lord in prayer as never before.

And then the telephone rang. It was a woman who was not

a Christian and whom we scarcely knew. She said, 'I know where your daughter is. I have come out to dinner having promised not to tell you, but something is prompting me to ring you. She is at my apartment with my husband. If you want you could go and try to persuade her to come home. I think she needs you.' Relief flooded through my whole being and that of the whole family. I went to fetch my daughter. It was not the end of the story, but it was the start of a time of reconciliation as we became aware of how much we had asked of her and how much she had struggled between two worlds. Looking back, I thank God for her courage and fortitude and for holding on to the hand of the Lord even through what sometimes seemed like the valley of the shadow of death. None of our family will ever forget that day. Once again our lives swung round as if on a hinge. It certainly changed our family prayer life for ever. In the days to come Anita and I gave over our mornings to prayer together, and what great times they were – ministering to God in this desert time. I dusted off an old guitar I had put away and we began to sing to Jesus together. The memory of those days is very sweet. Habakkuk says:

'Though the fig tree does not bud
and there are no grapes on the vines,
though the olive crop fails
and the fields produce no food . . .
yet will I rejoice in the Lord,
I will be joyful in God my Saviour.'

(Hab 3:17–18)

I will write more of this in a later chapter. For now let me say that the walls of our family prayer altar had been broken down, and we needed to build them up. We had forgotten to pray together as a couple or as a family for years on end, but this event changed everything. From that day on a week has never gone by without our gathering together before God in prayer; it has become our passion. Nor would any of our children question the usefulness of this. They have seen with their own eyes the effect of desperate prayer, and they would not do without it. Later on, our daughter came right back into the ways of God as he met her powerfully. But that is another story.

This experience of praying the desperate prayer of Hannah for her child had the unexpected effect of catapulting us into praying desperate prayers for our nation. As we experienced the fact that God answers heartfelt prayer for a teenager who is lost, so we began to mourn for the thousands of children and teenagers in the land who are starving for want of hearing the word of the Lord. We began, with the help of John Mulinde, incidentally, to turn our hearts towards the nation in which God had placed us. We began to be burdened and to plead for the nation in the same way as we had learnt to do for our own children. But this is to be the subject of the next chapter as we turn to Joel and hear how he received a burden for a nation.

You may feel that you need to get alone with God and pour out your heart for the particular situation of sterility that you are facing, with groaning and crying, just as Hannah did. As you do this, and as you see answers from God, I invite you to use the same passion, the same urgency, the same desperation to catch what the Holy Sprit is saying about the town, about the city, about the nation in which you find yourself.

THE STORY OF JOEL

'Even now,' declares the Lord, 'return to me with all your heart, with fasting and weeping and mourning.'

Rend your heart and not your garments. Return to the Lord your God, for he is gracious and compassionate, slow to anger and abounding in love, and he relents from sending calamity. Who knows? He may turn and have pity and leave behind a blessing – grain offerings and drink offerings for the Lord your God.

Blow the trumpet in Zion, declare a holy fast, call a sacred assembly. Gather the people, consecrate the assembly, bring together the elders, gather the children, those nursing at the breast. Let the bridegroom leave his room and the bride her chamber. Let the priests, who minister before the Lord, weep between the temple porch and the altar. Let them say, 'Spare your people, O Lord. Do not make your inheritance an object of scorn, a byword among the nations. Why should they say among the peoples, "Where is their God?"'

Then the Lord will be jealous for his land and take pity on his people. The Lord will reply to them: 'I am sending you grain, new wine and oil, enough to satisfy you fully; never again will I make you an object of scorn to the nations . . .' (Joel 2:12–19)

8

Fervent Prayer for a Nation

'"Deep calls to deep" . . . Prayer – protracted prayer, groaning prayer, fasting prayer, weeping prayer, speechless prayer – belongs to those initiated into a spirit of prayer, that is, into "praying in the holy Ghost". To the uninstructed, terms like these mean "works". But, praying friend, faint not; such critics may yet learn. In the language of Horatius Bonar it may be said of protracted, groaning, speechless prayer, "it is the way the master went, should not the servant tread it still?"'

(Leonard Ravenhill)[1]

'God has been pleased to constitute prayer to be an antecedent to the bestowment of mercy; and he is pleased to bestow mercy in consequence of prayer as though he were prevailed on by prayer. When the people of God are stirred up to prayer, it is the effect of his intention to show mercy; therefore he pours out the spirit of grace and supplication.'

(Jonathan Edwards)[2]

---

1 Leonard Ravenhill, *Revival Praying* (Bethany, 1962) p. 53.

2 Jonathan Edwards, quoted in John Piper, *A Hunger for God* (IVP, 1997) p. 174.

I have said that we live in a *kairos* alarm clock moment when God is waking up the church as never before to pray. Those who have eyes to see observe that, on every continent, we are witnessing a spiritual phenomenon that is completely new. It comes with the advent of Internet communication, and is fascinating to observe. For example, in France for the past several years God has been calling Christians to pray with greater intensity. Then in the year 2001 it seemed as if the Holy Spirit sovereignly called people all around the world to pray for France for the forty days before Easter. By different means people got to hear of the 'France 2001' website, one of two organisations promoting and serving the project. The website was visited by people as far afield as Malaysia, Vietnam and Brazil. Denominational heads called their churches to pray for France during that time. By the end of the period, France 2001 estimated that as many as two million people in the world had been praying for France.

We realised that no human agency could have organised this. It is this kind of phenomenon that causes Peter Wagner, a canny observer of what the Spirit is doing in the church worldwide, to make the following remarks: 'The modern prayer movement began around 1970. True, it had been burning brightly in Korea for some decades previously, but it was around 1970 that it started to spread world-wide. In recent years the expansion of the prayer movement has been exponential . . . Flames of prayer are being lit in virtually every denomination on every continent. Pastors are giving prayer a higher priority, children are praying fervently, prayer movements and prayer ministries are proliferating, theological seminaries are introducing courses on prayer and even secular magazines have been featuring cover stories about prayer.'[3]

---

[3] Peter Wagner in his Foreword to Dutch Sheets, *Intercessory Prayer* (Regal Books, 1996).

John Piper, from a different theological stream, remarks similarly, 'The return to prayer at the end of the twentieth century is a remarkable work of God. It is full of hope for the awakening of the church and the finishing of the Great Commission.'[4]

It is in this context that we come to the next on our list of intercessors – the prophet Joel. Joel is the prophet who authored the famous phrases 'blow the trumpet in Zion . . . sound the alarm . . . the day of the Lord is coming'. He was also responsible for the heart-stopping promise, 'And afterwards, I will pour out my Spirit on all people. Your sons and daughters will prophesy.' The prophecy was fulfilled at least in part on the day of Pentecost. No one knows exactly when he prophesied. It was either in the ninth century BC or perhaps in the days after the exile in the sixth century. But the message is not significantly affected by the date. Joel sees a massive locust plague and severe drought affecting the country as harbingers of the 'great and terrible day of the Lord'. Confronted with this crisis he calls everyone – young and old, priests and people, women and men – to repent.

There are moments in the life of a nation when this kind of preaching is called for. In France in December 1999, two events happened which shook the country to the core. The first was a storm which devastated and destroyed whole forests on the night of 26 December. No fewer than 300 million trees in that beautiful country were blown down in a single night, putting out the electricity to half a million homes. The second event was an oil spill which fetched up on the Brittany and Normandy beaches, creating havoc for the fishing and tourist industries.

In that context it was possible to read the first verses of Joel 2 with some seriousness. I remember doing a radio programme in Paris on 12 January 2000 with the theme of the

---

[4] John Piper, *Let the Nations Be Glad* (Baker Books, 1993).

first chapter of Joel 1: 'Has anything like this ever happened in your days or in the days of your forefathers? Tell it to your children, and let your children tell it to their children, and their children to the next generation. What the locust swarm has left the great locusts have eaten; what the great locusts have left, the young locusts have eaten' (Joel 1:2–4).

Every night the television screens of the country were filled with updates, seemingly ever more devastating, of the event, so the nation relived it day after day. It was in this context that several hundred churches 'just happened' to have called two prayer events. One was a night of prayer on the 31 December 1999, the eve of the new millennium, and the second was a forty-day fast for the first forty days of the year 2000.

The events preceding the fast certainly concentrated the minds of French Christians; and so it was that we met with a thousand people in a large church in central Paris for New Year's Eve, and thereafter we watched in some awe as more and more churches responded to the call to forty days of prayer and fasting for the first forty days of the year 2000. In the end over 500 churches and groups signed up for the event – which for France is striking. It ended in a national day for leaders of repentance and reconciliation. It was a time to 'proclaim a solemn assembly'. We don't know what the fruit of this will be. Sometimes, paradoxically, we have to admit that things can seem worse! We can lament with Jeremiah 8:20: 'The harvest is past, the summer has ended, and we are not saved.' But we also know we are in a long-term process. Jeremiah's reaction was to continue to cry out: 'Is there no balm in Gilead? Is there no physician there?' (Jer 8:22). The reaction of the French intercessors was to press on in prayer, with periods of prayer and fasting for the nation being called three years running by hundreds of churches. And we believe that, slowly but surely, the spiritual atmosphere is changing.

Joel's lessons for intercessors

First of all, Joel believes God is speaking through national disasters, and his message is – repent. It is as if he says, 'Get your eyes wide open to see events of national drama as the Lord's warning.' Early in the new millennium Britain was hit by hitherto unheard-of flooding, freak and terrible rail crashes and then foot and mouth disease. Fields were filled with the burning carcasses of livestock. An attempt was made in Britain to call a national day of prayer and fasting. Was this theologically correct or was Joel's event a one-off, unique occasion when God spoke through natural disaster? My answer is that if you look at the prophets Isaiah, Jeremiah and Ezekiel they certainly view history as being used by God to call a nation back to him. And Jesus, commenting on the big news item of his day – the tower of Siloam which fell on eighteen people – said, 'I tell you . . . unless you repent, you too will all perish' (Lk 13:5).

Second, Joel is urgent. He realises that there is not all the time in the world; it's a matter of urgency. Through him the Lord says, 'Return to me with all your heart, with fasting and weeping and mourning. Rend your heart and not your garments. Return to the Lord your God, for he is gracious and compassionate, slow to anger and abounding in love, and he relents from sending calamity' (Joel 2:12).

In our day we too can have the sense that there is a time of visitation, a time when the destiny of a nation hangs in the balance. Many prophetic voices are saying that the time is now for Europe. We are living in a time of a great worldwide harvest which is coming, and which is already present in different countries. Is it the will of God that the continent which gave birth to the Reformation will be left behind in this worldwide ingathering? The Reformation may be a dead issue for many but there was a time when men gave their lives – you can see them chiselled in stone in Geneva. The truth of the Reformation lives in the hearts of millions of Christians throughout the world because men seized the time with great courage. I believe that 'now is the time' to pray urgently like Joel.

Third, Joel's prayer is heartfelt – it is an affair of the heart. It is a matter for repentance and weeping. 'Return to me with all your heart . . . Rend your heart and not your garments.' Tearing one's clothes was a sign of grief. In 2 Samuel 1:11, David tears his clothes when he hears of Saul's death. Jacob tears his clothes when learning of Joseph's supposed death (Gen 37:34). It's almost a natural expression of the heart, unless it becomes a religious rite; and this is what it had become in Joel's day. So many good things can become mere rituals in our day too, and the intercessor will do well to check his heart almost daily. For example, speaking in tongues, falling under the anointing or singing worship songs. If these things lose the heart, then the prophet might say, 'Speak English, don't speak in tongues. Stand up for Jesus, don't fall over. Say what's on your heart, don't sing what's on someone else's.' The fact is that the Lord has always been looking for a people who would be whole-hearted. There is a sweet promise in Deuteronomy 4:29, 'You will find [God] if you look for him with all your heart.'

Joel says, 'Rend your heart and not your garments.' How do we rend our hearts? When I was first teaching this message, I met a man who had just had quadruple bypass surgery! He showed me the long, zip-like, dramatic scar on his chest and I realised the life-changing experience he had had. He said that after the operation he was like a new man. Rending your heart here is that groaning brokenness that we know when we hear of some tragedy that could perhaps have been avoided. For example, when the news came in to our church office recently that a young bride's new husband had been killed in a flying accident, I groaned and cried out in pain, and my colleague Francis said, 'I had exactly the same reaction when I heard the news.' We were 'rending our hearts'. Similarly, for our nations, we are to rend our hearts before the Lord.

Fourth, Joel is calling the people to weep and mourn. We have seen that God is pouring out his spirit of prayer around the world, and that often this is accompanied by weeping. In Africa, in Korea, in China, in South America, we see this heartfelt prayer which often includes tears. I remember asking a church in central Brazil how many of the congregation were in the habit of weeping when they prayed. Around eighty per cent of the church put up their hands to say that was their experience. When I was involved in preaching to the Chinese church that meets on Sunday afternoon in the church building in Belleville, Paris, I noted, at the time of the invitation, the tear-stained faces of those coming forward to repent. It is, as I have said, like a 'gift' or an 'anointing'. You can't drum it up, and when you've got it you certainly can't shake it off, nor should you. But if you haven't got it, you can ask for it. In the last century, the story goes, the Salvation Army were having difficulty bearing any fruit in France. Two missionaries sent a telegram to General Booth asking what to do. Days and weeks went by, until at last the old leader and founder of the movement replied. The two workers eagerly tore open the message. What would their founder's wise advice be? What strategy of open-air or music evangelism would he recommend for their hard field of action? When they opened the telegram they found it contained just two words: 'Try tears.'

If we compare notes with Hannah, Nehemiah, Jeremiah, Paul and Jesus we will find the same thing. This is, I believe, part of the 'spirit of supplication' of which Zechariah speaks: 'And I will pour out on the house of David and the inhabitants of Jerusalem a spirit of grace and supplication. They will look on me, the one they have pierced, and they will mourn for him as one mourns for an only child, and grieve bitterly for him as one grieves for a firstborn son. On that day the weeping in Jerusalem will be great . . . The land will mourn, each clan by itself, with their wives by themselves: the clan of the house of David and their wives' (Zech 12:10–12).

This weeping over sins, and particularly over 'the one they have pierced', is important. The intercessor senses the way the whole nation has turned away from God. He also knows that it is because of this rebellion that Christ came and gave up his life. He is aware of the agony and is deeply regretting the rejection of the only Son of God. He is fearing for the future, and knows that the nation deserves judgement. He is crying out that God would come, not in judgement but in mercy. He knows that the only hope is for mercy. As Joel says, 'Who knows? He may not turn and have pity and leave behind a blessing – grain offerings and drink offerings for the Lord your God.'

Joel is calling on the people to mourn and therefore to repent, but also to plead: 'Let the priests, who minister before the Lord, weep between the temple porch and the altar. Let them say, "Spare your people, O Lord. Do not make your inheritance an object of scorn, a byword among the nations."' The same call is found in Nehemiah, which we will look at when we come to the vital subject of identificational repentance. For the moment, we can see that it is a biblical principle to identify with the sin of your nation. We are not called to point the finger, but to intercede, to identify, to weep, to rend our hearts . . . even to stop eating.

I remember when I first went to France asking a 'father' of a missionary society what he felt was the key for France. He looked at me and replied, 'We find we can't get much done in France without tears . . . and fasting.'

And so, fifth, we see that Joel is gathering the people together for a period of corporate fasting. Edith Schaeffer said, 'Is fasting a bribe to get God to pay more attention to the petitions? No, a thousand times no. It is simply a way to make clear that we sufficiently reverence the amazing opportunity to ask help from the everlasting God, the creator of the universe, to choose to put everything aside and concentrate on worshipping, asking for forgiveness, and making our requests known – considering His help more important than anything we could do ourselves, in our own strength and with our own ideas.'[5]

It is with this in mind that we can understand the call of Joel. He joins Hannah and Daniel and Nehemiah and Jesus in calling the people to fast.

The easy yoke of fasting

This is a sweet discipline of intimacy with God that the Holy Spirit is bringing back on to the agenda. Fasting, for Jesus, was not an optional extra (he famously said, '*When* you fast . . .'). For Jesus, fasting was also the weapon that would cut free those who were bound and oppressed ('This kind comes out only through prayer with fasting'). For Daniel, fasting kept him sharp and keen when those around him were dulled by the rich foods and wines of the king. Nehemiah and Esther, after fasting, gained access to the king and to his favour. So we can say that fasting is the master key to unlock doors which otherwise remain shut. And in the twenty-first century, God is giving special enabling to do it. He woos us and draws us to do it, and then gives us the strength to carry on fasting, giving energy where normally we would give up. My experience in the last few years is that in times of God-ordained fast, God can give a desire to fast that can diminish greatly our desire for food. This is what I call the 'grace' of fasting. It is as if your hunger for God increases and your hunger for food diminishes.

---

[5] Edith Schaeffer in John Piper, *op cit*, p. 209.

One thing that can help us is the sense that a whole community is being called to fast for the nation. Jesus encouraged private fasting, but Joel encouraged corporate, community fasting. It is not either/or, but both/and. For three years we had times of community partial fasting for France over periods of forty days. My experience is that the solidarity with others is a great grace, and it helps me to sense an enabling and a certain ease in fasting. My testimony is that in such times the word of God, the Bible, becomes particularly real and preciously nourishing. There is also an authority and a sharpness that only comes through fasting.

Another motivating factor for fasting is the longing for the intervention of God. In his excellent book on fasting, *A Hunger for God*, John Piper argues that fasting is there to show that we have more hunger for God and his presence and his intervention than for food. He also adds this: 'Fasting is the physical expression of heart-hunger for the coming of Jesus. Jesus said: "The days will come when the Bridegroom is taken away from them and then they will fast." So Jesus connects Christian fasting with our longing for the return of the Bridegroom. Therefore, one of the most important meanings of Christian fasting is to express the hunger of our hearts for the coming of our king.'[6]

One man at the forefront of a call for fasting on behalf of America has been the unlikely figure of Bill Bright, founder of Campus Crusade for Christ, or 'Agape' as it is now known. His book *America's Call to Fast and Pray* has had a profound influence and he sums up his convictions thus: 'It will take nothing short of the supernatural to stem the tide of judgement devastating our land. I believe that nothing else can compare with the supernatural power released when we fast and pray.' He is echoing the conviction resounding like a trumpet from the pages of Joel's prophecy. Lest this

[6] John Piper, *op cit*, p. 70.

emphasis on fasting seem beyond us, Joel marries it with a majestically motivating insight, which we turn to now.

This sixth key to Joel's intercession is that he is interceding in the presence of the glory of God. He says, 'Return to the Lord your God, for he is gracious and compassionate, slow to anger and abounding in love, and he relents from sending calamity' (Joel 2:13). This is to say that Joel is, like Hannah before him, standing in the presence of God, holding on to him like Jacob, persisting like Abraham. He is remembering the character of God, which is the glory of God, like Moses when he said, 'Show me your glory.' This factor of remembering the glory of God is an important part of the dynamic of intercession. It changes the prayer from the realms of the impossible into the grace-filled realm of communion with God. This is not to say there is no effort, no sweat or tears; but there is an enabling, and there is mercy! So this is intercession based on the precious, gentle, loving character of God. Even in a context of judgement, there is this friendship and confidence.

There are two other keys to Joel's intercession and they are so important that it seems appropriate to treat them in two separate chapters. One is the question of whether God deals with nations, and if so, how can we pray for the prophetic destiny of a nation? Before that, however, we will examine another crucial aspect of Joel's prayer life. This is for many a forgotten aspect of the discipline of intimacy, but it is one that the Holy Spirit is bringing back to remembrance. I'm referring to the call for whole families to pray together, and to restore the 'family prayer altar'.

9
Rebuilding the Family Prayer Altar

'It was a new experience just to hear a thousand women and girls praying aloud at one time. The sound rose and fell like the roar of the sea or the wind in the forest.'
(G. H. Laing, describing the revival in India in 1905)[1]

'A young Muslim girl had become a Christian and in that room was given such a burden for her unsaved relatives as just broke the hearts of those who listened . . . a group of young girls had come many miles and each girl brought a hungry heart. It was terrible to watch the agony on their faces.'
(Basil Miller describing the Indian revival of 1909)[2]

'Gather the people, consecrate the assembly; bring together the elders; gather the children, those nursing at the breast. Let the bridegroom leave his room and the bride her chamber. Let the priests who minister before the Lord, weep between the temple porch and the altar.

---

1 G. H. Laing, describing the revival in India in 1905, quoted in Brian Mills, *Preparing for Revival* (Kingsway, 1990) p. 124.
2 Basil Miller, *Praying Hyde, Ambassador* (Emerald International, 2000) p. 76.

Let them say, "Spare your people, O Lord. Do not make your inheritance an object of scorn, a byword among the nations. Why should they say among the peoples, 'Where is their God?'"'

(Joel 2:16–17)

One of the compelling composants of Joel's account is that he has an understanding of the role of the family in prayer and in revival. He will later prophesy of Pentecost that in the last days 'your sons and your daughters will prophesy, your old men will dream dreams, your young men will see visions' (v. 28). This is a climate when the whole family is going to be caught up in a move of God. I believe we are living in a time when whole families can be baptised with a spirit of prayer. Joel says we are to call the newly-weds, the elderly, the infants and the babies. No one is left out, not among the priests or the people. I believe this is a profound challenge to many of us in the West. It can be interpreted as a call to re-establish the family altar. Is this possible in post-modern Europe? We think yes! But it is not necessarily easy.

I have already told our family's story in Chapter 8. In a time of crisis we were helped by an African. As we got to know him, John Mulinde from Uganda began to share with us his feelings when, as an African, he first began to travel and to meet Christians in Europe. He gently told us of his surprise, when welcomed as a guest into Christian homes, to find that there was almost never any prayer as a feature of family life. Sometimes the husband or wife was not a Christian; sometimes it was the teenage children who were not. But even in homes where every member of the family was a Christian, prayer was often seemingly absent. Even when children were young, it seemed, prayer was not a part of the warp and woof of a Christian home. 'My house shall be a house of prayer for all nations' was not something that applied to the European Christian home. And yet for John it was not as if the children in Europe were safe in the kingdom of God; they were just as much at risk as those in Uganda, but in a different, more subtle way.

John came from Uganda, the 'pearl of Africa', where under two successive dictatorships – that of Amin and then that of Obote – the country had effectively suffered rape. Christians had been on the run; their children had been in terrible danger. They had discovered that the only hope was desperate, Hannah-like intercessory prayer, continuously, day and night, with fasting. The testimony of Ugandan Christians is that through this God intervened and changed their country around. It is now relatively stable, with a God-fearing president, Musoveni. And it is one of the few, if not the only African country, where the progression of AIDS has not only slowed down, but rates of infection have diminished.

John told us that he felt the children of England and France were just as much in danger from unbelief, drugs and a godless lifestyle as the Ugandans had been. The difference was, here the Christians were sleeping. There was little prayer, and few homes were houses of prayer. As we listened to him, we felt how right he was. 'How much time do the Ugandan Christians spend praying as families?' we asked. 'And how often each week?'

'Every day for about an hour in the evenings,' was his reply. Our jaws dropped, and we immediately began to argue the impossibility of such a lifestyle in Europe. We began to ask 'what if?' questions.

'What if work keeps the parents out late?'

'Then the one who is there, usually the mother, will gather the children.'

'What if there are teenage friends present who are not Christians?'

'Well, they don't have to take part, but we find that often the prayer time is interesting and exciting, so teenage guests who are not yet Christians want to join in, and soon they will become Christians!'

Hmmm!

After the incident I related earlier when one of our daughters went missing, we took stock. This had happened in a home where communication was relatively good and open. We realised we were in a war.

In the past, we had sometimes become aware of the level of spiritual warfare that we were engaging in. Paul says, 'For our struggle is not against flesh and blood, but against the rulers, against the authorities, against the powers of this dark world and against the spiritual forces of evil in the heavenly realms . . . pray in the Spirit on all occasions with all kinds of prayers and requests' (Eph 6:12, 18).

Peter says: 'Your enemy the devil prowls around like a roaring lion looking for someone to devour. Resist him' (1 Pet 5:8). Without being fixated on the demonic, Anita and I realised we were in a battle, a battle in which the only hope was prayer. We began to pray together as a couple in a completely new, heartfelt way. And we talked with our children about this fact that our 'family prayer altar' had been broken down. Would they be interested in helping us build it up again? The answer was a definite yes. This was partly because of the fact that they all realised the fragility of our situation, and partly because the experience of praying together had made them aware that God answers prayer. Our next step was to discuss when we would meet and for how long. It is no good taking an impulsive decision to pray together as a family NOW! That is a formula guaranteed to cause frustration among teenagers who may have other projects. But to discuss when would be the best time for everyone in the future is to remove the pressure, and also to raise the level of importance of the project.

Our family pretty soon agreed that Sunday nights would be a good time. In France it is not part of the church culture to have an evening service, which was a help to us in finding a time. What is more, Sunday night is the time when families regroup and get themselves organised for the week to come. We agreed to eat together and then afterwards to worship and to pray for around an hour.

Eating together as a complete family is a precious privilege that some reading this may need to rediscover. Sometimes when I have taught this material, people have objected: 'Well, we never eat together, and we never really see each other to talk, so how will we do this?' My question in that case is, 'Is this right?' It is said that one of the causes of anorexia today is the demise of the experience of families eating together. So when we do gather together, the television in the eating area needs to be turned off and programmes videoed. This is because the experience of eating together first is going to affect the experience of praying together. This is because it is impossible to pray together effectively, wholeheartedly, if relationships are out of sorts. Sometimes this time will need to be used to put things right.

People have sometimes said to me, 'Well, we could never do this as my brother hates my sister and she hates him! It would never work in our family.' Seriously? If this is the case I ask again, 'Is this right?' Is it right to allow festering relationships to drag on week after week without reconciliation and forgiveness and love being restored? There have been times when, if I have felt that things are not right in the home and there is a bad atmosphere, I have addressed it at this meal time, sometimes with unexpected consequences. I remember once, shortly after we had sat down, saying, 'Right, I am not happy that you children never lift a finger to help your mother in the kitchen. I will not have you treating your mother with such disrespect and I will not have you treating this place like a hotel!' I was quite proud of my speech until one of my children replied, 'Well, you never do anything to clear up in the kitchen either, Dad.' I turned with a shocked look to my wife for support. She, always a tiger for the truth, helpfully said, 'That is in fact true.' Now it was my turn to choose. Either I could send my child off to bed for being so cheeky, or I could apologise and commit myself to changing my behaviour too. I have in fact often had to apologise to my children. The Bible says, 'Fathers, do not exasperate your children' (Eph 6:4). I think that one way not to exasperate them is to apologise quickly when in the wrong.

Another equally important thing is to be a priest in your own home, and lead your whole family to God in prayer. In this current climate, when God is pouring out his Spirit on all flesh, on sons and daughters, as Joel says, I am convinced we need to see things in a new way. Your children who love God may well be exasperated – not if you do lead them to pray, but if you don't.

Anyway, at these meal times we will have a sweet, deep, often fun time of communicating and listening to one another, finding out what is on each other's programme for the coming week and later on interceding for any demanding struggles coming up.

Prepare for war!

When we decide to start all over again and promote prayer in our home, it is wise if we realise we may be in for a struggle. First, there will inevitably be a host of 'worthy' interruptions. Suddenly the children will remember vital bits of homework that 'have' to be done before they can pray. Adults will remember phone calls that 'have' to be made. Family and friends will ring in and even if the voicemail is switched on, everyone will suddenly be 'expecting a call'! What is more, rows may unexpectedly break out. If there have been any unresolved disagreements over the past week, they will need to be resolved, or the Holy Spirit may be grieved and just not show up! All these things are inevitable, and we have to take a deep breath and get through them. We may well need to ask forgiveness from one another. But where there is a will, gradually, a pattern of prayer can be established.

Just as a lighter example of this, I remember reading a story James Dobson tells of a family with young children who had decided to get some 'quality time' together. As a big treat, they decided to drive to a theme park an hour and a half away. As often happens the small children chose this day to be particularly obnoxious to one another, squabbling and hitting each other for the first long thirty minutes of the car trip. After repeated warnings and pleadings, Dad pulled the car over, took them out and spanked them both and said, 'If I hear another peep out of either of you for the next hour, you will get exactly the same treatment and we will go straight home.'

'Yes, Daddy!' was the muted reply.

The next hour passed in silence as the children watched the sixty minutes tick by on the digital clock. Mum too sat in silence on this 'quality day out'. At last, the sixtieth minute clicked past and one of the children said, 'Dad, can I say something?'

'Yes.' (Through gritted teeth.)

'Well, when you took us out of the car to spank us back there, my shoe fell off and it's still there in the lay-by.'

Now it was the mother who, driven to despair by the loss of the only decent pair of shoes the boy possessed, turned round and hit the back seat like a crazy lady. So ended the family's 'quality day out'!

When we institute the family prayer altar, we may be faced with similar tests, but if we remember that our struggle is not against flesh and blood, our capacity to persevere may be enhanced! As E. M. Bounds says, 'Satan has suffered so much by good praying that all his wily, shrewd and ensnaring devices will be used to cripple its performances.'[3] We need to remember this and be encouraged.

When we get down to pray, we try as far as possible to create an atmosphere of faith. This may happen by lighting a candle, if that seems appropriate for you. I remember hearing the testimony of a Jewish child who came from a violent background. She said the only times in her childhood that she remembers feeling peace, however remotely, was when the Sabbath evening candles were lit for the family meal. Then she knew that this at least was a special time.

Then a most vital ingredient: we will try always to read the word of God and discuss it, often from a new translation, and, as it happens, always read by our youngest child. We have so enjoyed her pronunciations of obscure names, that many of them can now only be pronounced for us in 'Jemimah's way'. The word of God should penetrate our homes in the West in a new way. The book of Deuteronomy speaks so clearly of the care a father should take to keep the word of God before his family. 'And these commandments that I give you today are to be upon your hearts. Impress them on your children. Talk about them when you sit at home and when you walk along the road, when you lie down and when you get up . . . Write them on the door-frames of your houses and on your gates' (Deut 6:6–8). In the light of this, I believe the least we can do is to gather regularly as a family to listen to and discuss the word of God. The passage goes on, 'When the Lord your God brings you into the land he swore to your fathers . . . a land with large, flourishing cities . . . and houses filled with all kinds of good things you did not provide . . . then when you eat and are satisfied, be careful that you do not forget the Lord, who brought you out of Egypt, out of the land of slavery . . . for the Lord your God, who is among you, is a jealous God' (vv. 10–14).

---

[3] E. M. Bounds, *A Treasury of Prayer* (Bethany House, 1961), p. 25.

Many of us have come to a point where, as a family, we have almost 'forgotten the Lord'. One way to remember him is to bring his word back to be the subject of our discussions, and the application of his word the subject of our prayers. This is particularly true when our children are teenagers or young adults wanting (almost inevitably) to go clubbing[4] or whatever the current equivalent may be. Every activity, however apparently shady, can be subjected to the light of the word of God. We have often found our discussions at the table to be illuminated by our reading a little later, and this is a lesson that our children will never forget.

When we gather for prayer we will want to begin, probably, with worship. If some members of the family lead worship, get them to prepare their instruments and their music for this time and to be ready to lead the whole family without apology into worship. It is good if the time of prayer does not turn into a time of acrimonious rehearsal as the particular rhythm of a song is fiercely debated – a pretty sure atmosphere killer. One key is to think ahead. A wise father will organise music and words for songs, and so on, or get one of the family to plan some CD tracks to help you sing to the Lord and 'build a throne of praise' at home. This is such a precious thing to do and can affect the atmosphere of victory and bring the presence of Jesus into your house. He is after all the One who is enthroned on the praises of his people (Ps 22:3, AV). Remarkable things can happen as we bring the struggles of our different family members to God and proclaim his glory over them.

A time of prayer as a family can well be as touching as that

---

[4] Clubbing is a worldwide phenomenon of the early twenty-first century involving, essentially, dancing all night. It can be neutral, but may involve drugs and casual relationships which do untold damage. As it usually is at its most appealing on a Saturday night, it may affect a teenager's sharpness when in church the next morning!

proposed by Joel. It is not necessarily a formal, empty time but, as Joel describes, it can be heartfelt, pleading prayer throughout the family. O let our families catch this!

Our conviction in the 'Intercession France' movement during these past years was that prayer was catching on around the country, churches were being impacted with the spirit of prayer and there was a sense of something coming to birth. But even in this context we felt that the enemy of our souls would not be too troubled if prayer could be confined to the churches. However, if every Christian home became a fire of prayer burning; if every home became a house of prayer for all the nation and for all nations; if all across the country fires were lit wherever you looked – then he would really be in trouble! And who knows? God may hear the cry of his people crying to him day and night and choose to send mercy and revival to that needy land. That prophet of prayer Zechariah has an interesting element in his picture of a prayer revival: 'And I will pour out . . . a spirit of grace and supplication. They will look on me, the one they have pierced, and they will mourn for him as one mourns for an only child, and grieve bitterly for him as one grieves for a firstborn . . . The land will mourn, each clan by itself, with their wives by themselves; the clan of the house of David and their wives, the clan of the house of Nathan and their wives, the clan of the house of Levi and their wives, the clan of Shimei and their wives' (Zech 12:10–13). This passage again suggests that whole families are to catch this spirit of prayer, and that it will be characterised by tears and earnestness and urgency.

So the prayer time of a family can proceed with energy, bringing before God different situations for which family members are burdened. As Joel says, 'Why should they say among the peoples, "Where is their God?"' Bring the situations of defeat – friendships which are threatened, peer pressure which is becoming unsupportable – to the Lord.

Sometimes in situations of sickness or struggle we have laid hands on one another, anointed one another with oil, and so forth. My point is that prayer in the home should be powerful – if anything, more powerful than prayer in the church. And as prayer in the church gets more powerful and full of authority, so should prayer in the home!

It is also good to pray for family members who are not Christians, with the same passion. Finally, it is good to widen the scope of family prayer to the nations. It is possible that different family members will be concerned for different situations; talk about them and bring them to Jesus.

Always try to end a family prayer time with praise and worship, leaving the burdens with Jesus. If we do this, the whole atmosphere in our family can gradually change and we can be a source of healing for others.

To sum up, here are ten steps to building a family prayer altar:

1. Be convinced of the need.
2. Call a family discussion and gain agreement and ownership (as far as is possible!). Dads (if there is one), become 'priests' to your family!
3. Decide on a regular, weekly time and place and length of time. Guard it jealously and, if there are guests, let them know that it is your family prayer time. Preferably try to keep this time clear of guests. If people press you to go out, let them know you have a prior date – with your children and with your God.
4. Be prepared for war! At least know that there may be opposition to your plans on the day.
5. Have a meal together and express love and forgiveness and family affection. Enjoy each other's company! Lighten up, be reconciled. Parents, ask your children to forgive you. Set an example. Dads, do not exasperate your children.

6. Light a candle and create atmosphere. Turn off the phones and television.
7. Get out the instruments and the songbooks.
8. Use a modern translation of the Bible and choose a book to follow together.
9. Discuss the battles each is going through and make them the subject for prayer. Bring to the family prayer time the 'spirit of prayer' that you have received.
10. Repeat steps 1–9 next week.

What if some of the family are not Christians?

My advice would be to suggest starting with those who are. If it is a question of a couple who are Christians and their children not, this is comparatively easy. Make the conversion of your children or step-children the subject of daily, heart-felt prayer together. Go through the teaching above together and put it into practice.

If it is a spouse who is not yet a Christian, more care and tact and winsomeness are needed. But it is still good to discuss it with your spouse and to ask if he or she would like to be present at the family prayer time, or if he or she would have any objection to it taking place. It is remarkable what occurs for those who ask, seek and knock.

What if the marriage is dysfunctional?

This is a more delicate and vital question. It is true that if an enthusiastic Christian wife or husband tries to stick family prayer on to a bleeding marriage, like a plaster over a terminal wound, it may not be appropriate. It will be just dressing a wound and not healing it. What may be needed is confession, forgiveness and a new start. If a married couple's intimate life is not working, it may be hypocritical to pray together: there is too much pain present. There needs at the very least to be communication about that area. However, my experience is that nothing is unhealable; that is to say, nothing is beyond the scope of the love of God. For one member of a partnership to suggest praying together may be to provoke communication about areas which either one may not be happy with. This is a necessary prelude to praying in unity together. So before calling a family conference, it may be good for a couple to go out on a date together, to discuss this project and gain agreement. Discuss your marriage together, discuss areas of dissatisfaction, grievance, and discuss the prayer proposal. This is of course the subject of a whole book, so suffice it to say here that this date and this discussion will be a good investment of time and money!

Aim for a family that is devoted rather than family devotions

I remember hearing John Wimber say once that he was never much good at family devotions, but that he felt his children had picked up the fact that he and his wife Carol were devoted to God. By this he meant that he had not been good at gathering his family to read the Bible, but that their house had been constantly open to those in need. His children had prayed with him for the sick and the demonised and seen them delivered right before their eyes in their home. If John had to choose, he would rather have that. Well, I would too! But I would say there must be coherence. A family that has a weekly prayer time, but whose home is not open to those in need of God, should examine their ways. All the above remarks about guarding the family prayer time assume that the family is ministering in the kingdom of God. The two go hand in hand. Let us learn to open our homes to the power of God in the place of prayer, and let us learn to open them to the poor in spirit and see the deliverance that God wants to bring to those around us!

ISAIAH'S STORY

For Zion's sake I will not keep silent, for Jerusalem's sake I will not remain quiet, till her righteousness shines out like the dawn, her salvation like a blazing torch. The nations will see your righteousness, and all kings your glory; you will be called by a new name that the mouth of the Lord will bestow. You will be a crown of splendour in the Lord's hand, a royal diadem in the hand of your God. No longer will they call you Deserted, or name your land Desolate. But you will be called Hephzibah, and your land Beulah; for the Lord will take delight in you, and your land will be married. As a young man marries a maiden, so will your sons marry you; as a bridegroom rejoices over his bride, so will your God rejoice over you.

I have posted watchmen on your walls, O Jerusalem; they will never be silent day or night. You who call on the Lord, give yourselves no rest, and give him no rest till he establishes Jerusalem and makes her the praise of the earth.

The Lord has sworn by his right hand and by his mighty arm: 'Never again will I give your grain as food for your enemies, and never again will foreigners drink the new wine for which you have toiled; but those who harvest it will eat it and praise the Lord, and those who gather the grapes will drink it in the courts of my sanctuary.'

Pass through, pass through the gates! Prepare the way for the people. Build up, build up the highway! Remove the stones. Raise a banner for the nations. The Lord has made proclamation to the ends of the earth: 'Say to the Daughter of Zion, "See, your Saviour comes! See, his reward is with him, and his recompense accompanies him."' They will be called the Holy People, the Redeemed of the Lord; and you will be called Sought After, the City No Longer Deserted. (Is 62:1–12)

10
Praying for the Nations

'There is no other city that has been at the centre of controversy for the past three thousand years like the small piece of real estate we know as Jerusalem. Founded by king David as his capital, this city of the great king, as it is known throughout history, is still the centre of national and international conflict in the twenty-first century. The number of prophecies and promises related to this city make it a jewel in the heart of many great religions in the world and the pivot of the historic fulfilment of Christian eschatology.'

(Miles Munroe)[1]

'The Catholic Church has experienced a revolution in her understanding of her relationship to the Jewish people. Since Vatican II, the teaching given concerning the Jewish people is radically different from that of previous centuries: the Jewish people are no longer the people cursed and rejected by God, but those of divine election . . . All Christian traditions are called to rediscover, through understanding the role of the Jewish people, their true eschatological hope.'

(Peter Hocken)[2]

---

[1] Dr Miles Munroe, Foreword to Tom Hess, *Pray for the Peace of Jerusalem*, p. vi, 2000.

[2] Peter Hocken, interview in *Embrase Nos Coeurs* magazine, March 2001. See also his book *The Glory and the Shame.*

Isaiah, thought to be the greatest of the writing prophets, began his ministry in 740 BC, the year that King Uzziah died. According to an unsubstantiated Jewish tradition, he was sawn in half during the reign of Manasseh. At the moment of his call, Isaiah 'saw the Lord'. He was someone who, like other intercessors we have considered, had an experience of the 'glory', a vision of the Lord, high and lifted up, with his robe filling the temple, and the temple filling up with smoke.

We pick up the prophet's writing in chapter 62, just after the beautiful messianic prophecy of Isaiah 61: 'The Spirit of the Sovereign Lord is on me, because the Lord has anointed me to preach good news.'

PART 1: PRAYING FOR ISRAEL

'For Zion's sake I will not keep silent, and for Jerusalem's sake, I will not remain quiet' (Is 62:1). The first thing we see in this passage is that Isaiah is praying for the people of God – for Zion and Jerusalem. The subject and burden of the intercessor are very important. Whatever else it may mean, the immediate application of this verse is that we are to pray for Israel and for Jerusalem. This is a subject that has caused controversy, but which those who discipline themselves to a life of intimacy with God will find themselves drawn to. I believe this is a work of the Holy Spirit. I myself began to understand this for the first time when in 1999 I was led to preach an expository series from Isaiah 40–66. In the light of current events, and also looking at the high concentration of Jewish people in the area of Paris where we were living, people who so love Israel and Jerusalem, I could not get away from the main and plain meaning of the texts about Zion and Jerusalem.

Two events that particularly encouraged many Christians to review their understanding of scriptures about Israel were the creation of the state of Israel in 1948, and the renewed presence of the Jewish people back in 'old' Jerusalem since the Six-Day War in 1967. What had been invisible and almost forgotten was suddenly visible, and since then has been at the heart of world events. Some of the motives behind the events of 11 September 2001 have again put Israel at the heart of world conflict.

When I talk about praying for Israel, I am not suggesting an uncritical stance towards the actions of the state of Israel. From the very beginning her actions have been questionable. The seeds of the problem are in the motto with which the modern campaign to found the state of Israel began. 'A land without a people for a people without a land'[3] was a catchy slogan, but neatly avoided the fact that the land was already full of people, namely Palestinians. Israel has certainly done wrong in trusting in tanks rather than turning in repentance towards the Lord. And so has the Palestinian Authority. As I write, the Israeli army is razing Palestinian homes, causing bitterness and suffering, and the Palestinian suicide bombers are killing and wounding Jewish civilians, leaving scars that will be difficult to heal. Both sides feel deeply that their actions are justified. I am not talking about an unquestioning acceptance of the actions of either side; rather I am talking about the people of Israel in the purposes of God into whom we (Gentiles) have been grafted and who have, according to Paul, 'experienced a hardening in part until the full number of the Gentiles has come in' (Rom 11:25).

It can be said that there have been in recent years two equal and opposite errors as regards Israel. For many years, due to the teaching of the Reformers, there has been a

---

[3] Quoted in Larry Collins and Dominique Lapierre, *O Jerusalem* (Steimatzky, 1972).

'theology of replacement', simply replacing Israel with the Christian church in the prophetic writings. When we read Isaiah 62 today we unconsciously do this; we read this passage as an injunction not to be silent in favour of the church. Since the creation of the state of Israel, however, there has been among some Christians an equal and opposite error – namely the substitution of the church by Israel; so that all the energies of some are poured into the promotion of a love for Israel, often at the expense of a love for the church. Sometimes this takes the form of the veneration of Israel and a frustration with the church for not taking the same view.

The balanced biblical position is a love and an intercession for both. We shall see this when we look at the practice of Paul. From him we shall see that the intercessor will pray energetically for the church and the equipping of the saints for the work of ministry; and also for the salvation of all Israel and the unblinding of the eyes of Israel and the removing of the veil.

To return to our passage, then, Isaiah is not first of all talking about the church; he has no concept of the church. He is saying: for Zion's sake, for Jerusalem's sake. It is on the walls of Jerusalem that he has set watchmen, and he exhorts them not to be silent. 'You who call on the Lord, give yourselves no rest, and give him no rest till he establishes Jerusalem and makes her the praise of the earth.' Isaiah prophesies about the restoration of Jerusalem in the beautiful passages in chapters 52, 54 and 60, which precede our text, and another example of a call to pray for Israel and Jerusalem can be found in Psalm 122:

Pray for the peace of Jerusalem:
'May those who love you be secure.
May there be peace within your walls and security
within your citadels.'

For the sake of my brothers and friends, I will say,
'Peace be within you.'
For the sake of the house of the Lord our God, I will
seek your prosperity.'

And also in Psalm 137:

If I forget you, O Jerusalem,
may my right hand forget its skill.
May my tongue cling to the roof of my mouth if I do
not remember you,
if I do not consider Jerusalem my highest joy.

In the year 2000, I went to Jerusalem for the first time and spent most of two weeks inside the city walls. If this is the 'house of the Lord', I must say it is a beautiful one. What a place! 'The city of our God.' We sensed the peace still present at that time, and we felt the tension beneath the surface, of course. We loved the Jewish people, and we loved the Palestinians, too. Perhaps because of living in France, we also loved the Arab quarter. We were stirred and awed at the Wailing Wall and in the extraordinarily impressive Jewish quarter. After you've seen Jerusalem, it seems there's no chance you'll forget it, although the psalmist knows that in time we may! As I walked round the walls I began to understand the target of Isaiah's prayer. And it can be ours too, this burden for his house, the church, and for his house, Jerusalem.

What helped me was the beautiful, balanced position of Paul, writing in Romans 9, 10 and 11 of his intercessor's burden both for Israel and for the church. He talks of the partial hardening of Israel that has happened (11:25). He talks of arousing unbelieving Israel to envy (11:13). And this is how he prays: his heart's desire and prayer to God is that they may be saved (Rom 10:1). He says he is in great sorrow and has unceasing grief in his heart for the sake of his brethren the Israelites. Those who draw near to God may find this sorrow coming upon them as they are drawn into what Paul elsewhere called the pains of childbirth or 'groans too deep for words'.

At the end of Romans 9, Paul repeatedly quotes Isaiah. He talks of the Gentiles being saved, but also of 'the remnant'. Later he makes his classic statement: 'And if they do not persist in unbelief, they will be grafted in, for God is able to graft them in again. After all, if you were cut out from an olive tree that is wild by nature, and contrary to nature were grafted into a cultivated olive tree, how much more readily will these, the natural branches, be grafted into their own olive tree! I do not want you to be ignorant of this mystery, brothers, so that you may not be conceited. Israel has experienced a hardening in part until the full number of the Gentiles has come in. And so all Israel will be saved' (11:23–26).

Paul sees a future for the church, but also a future for the remnant of Israel, the natural olive tree into which the Gentile church is grafted. And he talks about his commitment to praying for both.[4] Returning to Isaiah 62, we see how the intercessor prays to the Father for the righteousness of Jerusalem to shine forth like the dawn, and asks very precisely that her salvation (all Israel being saved?) will shine like a blazing torch. He takes up the theme again in verse 7, where he encourages us to go on giving God no rest until he 'establishes Jerusalem and makes her the praise of the earth'.

---

[4] Rob Richards, whose book *Has God Finished with Israel?* is a full treatment of this subject, says: 'My view is that you cannot have the Church without a believing Israel, Eph 3:6: "This mystery is that through the gospel the Gentiles are heirs *together with Israel,* members together of one body, and sharers together in the promise in Christ Jesus."'

Isaiah prophesies the comfort of God

Isaiah goes on to prophesy comfortable words and promises from the God of all comfort and consolation. He is filled with a spirit of prophecy in these verses. He says, 'You will be a crown of splendour in the Lord's hand, a royal diadem in the hand of your God. No longer will they call you Deserted, or name your land Desolate. But you will be called Hephzibah [My delight is in her].' As we have said before, the intercessor will find that as he is seated in the presence of God, in the glory of God, in the heavenly realms, he will gain prophetic insight into the future as the Spirit comes upon him. And often he will be aware of the compassion of God. It is the same as when John, in Revelation 1, was 'in the Spirit on the Lord's day . . . and I saw'. We are called to this prophetic proclamation. The content of Isaiah's prophecy is the future of Israel (or 'restoration of Israel') into whom the church is grafted.

'Your land will be married'

A burden for Isaiah was that the land would be called 'married' (v. 4). The idea of marriage brings with it thoughts of covenant, commitment, love, long term relationship, sacrifice and fruitfulness. When people are not ready for commitment, they are not ready to get married. Too many Christians abandon not only their first love for God, but also for the geographical land where he has placed them; many never experience it. One way to 'marry the land' is to care for it and tend it and not exploit it; to 'think ecologically' and to pray for organisations like the Arocha Trust, a Christian organisation working for the environment in fifteen different countries.[5]

Isaiah senses the blessing of people 'marrying the land'. When God's people are in the land covenanted to them by promise (Gen 12:7) the people and the land prosper as in a marriage. But when they are exiled, the land languishes and becomes desolate. We can 'marry' the land of Israel by praying for it. We can pray with constancy and compassion and commitment for its union with the Jewish people and its protection, for compassion to the poor to fill the land, and a love for God and a revelation of Christ.

God is also looking for Christians who will 'marry' the place where he has called us, loving our land, our city, our town – and not complaining about it. This is another aspect of Isaiah's discipline of intimacy and is increasingly needed by Christians today.

The ministry of the watchman

'I have posted watchmen on your walls, O Jerusalem; they will never be silent day or night' (v. 6). The watchmen on the walls of Jerusalem would look for the runner from the battle who brought the news of its outcome. In Ezekiel 3:17 the ministry of the watchman was also to give a warning if it was needed.

This ministry is costly and prophetic, but there is nothing to fear if it is exercised within the safety of submission to the spiritual leadership of the local church.

Ezekiel 33:1–7 is another passage for Christians who are serious about praying. Here the ministry also involves sounding a trumpet: 'If the watchman sees the sword coming and does not blow the trumpet to warn the people and the sword comes and takes the life of one of them, that man will be taken away because of his sin, but I will hold the watchman accountable for his blood. Son of man, I have

---

[5] For more, see 'Creation and Gospel', six teaching seminar CDs with Eugene Peterson and Peter and Miranda Harris, available from Regent College, Vancouver.

made you a watchman for the house of Israel' (Ezek 33:6–7).

It interests me that in these days, movements are springing up which take names like 'Watchmen Intercessors Trumpet Mission'. The idea for these exotic titles comes from texts such as this. Intercessors like Isaiah or Ezekiel, as well as discerning comfort, may also discern danger. Their job is to warn the people in such a way as to be understood.

Isaiah urges noisy prayer: 'Never be silent . . . call on the Lord . . .' and I would again encourage you to speak your prayers out loud. Thoughts often deepen as they are expressed, as mentioned in Chapter 4. This may appear but a detail but it does have a spiritual import. The fact is that for many, silent prayer results often in a blank mind, contentless prayer and even sleep. Perhaps this is why Isaiah says 'I will not be silent' and exhorts us: 'Give yourselves no rest.' In addition, his prayer is persistent; it is to happen day and night, not giving yourself rest, and giving him no rest until there is a breakthrough, 'until he establishes Jerusalem'.

Prepare the way

'Pass through, pass through the gates! Prepare the way for the people. Build up, build up the highway! Remove the stones. Raise a banner for the nations' (Is 62:10–12). Evidently Isaiah thought of himself as someone who was a 'preparer of the way'. These verses remind me of March for Jesus, which started with a cassette tape called 'Make Way'.[6] The intercessor may indeed be called to go through the

[6] Graham Kendrick and others started the 'Make Way' marches in the 1980s. Over twenty years this grew in impact until the last official March for Jesus Day in 2000 linked millions in scores of countries in what was hailed as the largest prayer meeting in the history of the world.

streets on prayer walks or on marches for Jesus to prepare the way for the spread of the gospel. From small beginnings March for Jesus spread to scores of nations, as thousands prayer-walked their cities on the same day, often in great numbers. In the year 2000, there were a million people marching on 'March for Jesus' Day in São Paulo, Brazil, alone.

What does it mean to prepare the way, to clear the stones? Tom Hess makes this verse the backbone of his book *Pray for the Peace of Jerusalem*.[7] He spends a hundred pages listing ten 'stones' that need removing in order to make way for the King. I have chosen some of them as key themes for action and for prayer.

1. Man's peace process

Despite the sacrificial efforts of some politicians, in some cases literally unto death,[8] and however much we may wish it to be otherwise, it is hard to see any process succeeding, so long as it excludes the Prince of Peace. We can go further and say that Islamic fundamentalists are sworn enemies of the Jewish state. So this is war on a deep spiritual level. It is to Jerusalem that the Prince of Peace will return (Acts 1:11) and the battle is to prevent his glorious return. Some would even say that just as the Holocaust was a battle to destroy the very people to whom he promised to return, so the battle rages to wrest Jerusalem, the place of his return, from that same people.

The true peace process is God's peace plan; true unity will come when Arabs and Jews together in Israel embrace the truth of the Prince of Peace and the word of God. And this we can pray for.

---

[7] Tom Hess, *Pray for the Peace of Jerusalem* (IVP, 2000).

[8] Both Presidents Anwar Sadat (Egypt) and Yitzak Rabin (Israel) have given their lives for this process.

2. The unbelief of the Arab world

I used to meet weekly with two young Arab men who came to faith in our church in Paris. I got to appreciate their humour, their hospitality, their gentleness. Tom Hess comments that 'the Arab people are the most friendly and hospitable people I have met anywhere in the world'.[9] It is true that when they accept Jesus they will become a tremendous blessing in the midst of the earth. But from the seventh century to this day Islam has had its own 'replacement theology', which most Arabs have embraced. Through the teachings of Muhammad, the Koran replaced the Bible, Mecca replaced Jerusalem, Ishmael replaced Isaac as the chosen, Islam replaced Judaism, the Muslim Arab nations replaced Israel. Around the golden Dome of the Rock on the temple mount in Jerusalem are written the words 'There is one God. His name is Allah and he has no son'. As we take our stand on the walls and watch; as we give him no rest; as we prepare the way and remove the stones, we can pray for the salvation of the Arab peoples. As we do so we will realise this is not a human issue, our struggle is not against flesh and blood. But things can change and radical conversions can happen. My two Arab friends in Paris are signs of it.[10]

3. Hardness of heart to the Jewish people

Replacement theology in the church may certainly have contributed to this.[11] We can and should pray for the salvation

---

[9] *Ibid*, p. 99.

[10] Isaiah has already prophesied a future vision of reconciliation in the Lord Almighty – 19:23–25, 'a blessing on earth' as this story above illustrates.

[11] Martin Luther's now shocking statements show the Protestant church has a heavy responsibility too. Here is an extract from one of his sermons: 'Burn their synagogues and schools; and what will not burn,

of the Jews. Charles Simeon, that great Anglican reformer, whose charitable trust is the patron of the church in Oxford that I now serve, traditionally gave his first financial gift of each new year to what is now known as the Church's Ministry among Jewish People (CMJ), because, as he said in his accompanying letter, 'the gospel is the power of salvation to the Jew first' (Rom 1:16). In our day it is interesting to note that when Israel became a state in 1948 there were only a few thousand messianic Jews in the world, that is, Jews who have become believers in Christ and belong to churches which still hold, in varying degrees, to the Jewish roots of the faith. Today the number is approximately 300,000.[12]

4. Lack of purity in the bride of Christ

'The bride making herself ready' is a key, and we can pray with energy for this. The consequence of this may be that Israel is provoked to positive envy. In Revelation we see a picture of the last days: 'For the wedding of the Lamb has come, and his bride has made herself ready. Fine linen, bright and clean, was given her to wear. (Fine linen stands for the righteous acts of the saints.)' (Rev 19:7–8). Paul suggests that he pursues his ministry in building the church, partly in order to provoke Israel to jealousy. He says: 'I am talking to you Gentiles . . . I make much of my ministry in the hope that I may somehow arouse my own people to envy and save some of them' (Rom 11:13–14). It follows that if the church is

---

Footnote 11 continued

bury with earth . . . Take away their prayer books, and Talmuds in which there is nothing but godlessness, lies, cursing and swearing. If I had power I would assemble their prominent men and demand that they prove we Christians do not worship God, under penalty of having their tongues torn out through the back of their neck.' In Stevens, *Strife Between Brothers* (Olive Press, 1979).

[12] Tom Hess, *op cit*, p. 144.

living out a lifestyle that corresponds to Christ; if there is reconciliation and the fragrance of Christ; if there is service of the poor and righteous deeds; if there is a clear testimony of changed lives, overflowing with the love of Jesus; then Jewish people who come into contact with such a community will become envious of the life and draw near to the light of the gospel and we may 'save some of them'. There was a French Jewish girl in our church in Paris who came to Christ recently, provoked as she was by the love she found among the Christians. Paul quotes Deuteronomy to say, 'I will make you envious by those who are not a nation' (Rom 10:19).

The problem is that often the church, because of her lack of purity, love and authority, does not arouse positive jealousy. She is anything but a bride who is ready for the Bridegroom. It is significant that the Pope in the year 2000 made it his business to ask forgiveness of the Jewish people for the sins of the church in years gone by. This 'identificational' repentance is part of the bride making herself ready. (I will say more of this later on in this chapter.) The intercessor can, with Isaiah, pray for the removal of this 'stone' of impurity, so that the road can be prepared. He can stand on the walls and give himself no rest, poised before the Lord and attentive to him.

We can prepare the way not only through prayer but also through loving the people around us. If the church has obscured the view, let us by our acts of love and by befriending the lost prepare the way. This is part of what being a watchman means. That is to say that we are not just warning the church but warning, perhaps with tears in our eyes, those in our families or in our circle of acquaintances; we are exhorting them to come to the Saviour. We need intercession, matched with interest in our neighbours; worship, hand in hand with witness; weeping in secret with wooing our friends; groaning with gaining a right to speak. In short, we need to be naturally supernatural and supernaturally natural as we prepare the way for the King.

PART 2: PRAYING FOR THE NATIONS

Two hundred years ago, William Blake wrote the following lines, which became a famous hymn:

And did those feet in ancient times
Walk upon England's mountains green?
And was the holy Lamb of God
In England's pleasant pastures seen?

And did the countenance Divine
Shine forth upon those clouded hills?
And was Jerusalem builded here,
Among those dark satanic mills?

. . . I will not cease from mental strife,
Nor shall my sword sleep in my hand,
Till we have built Jerusalem
In England's green and pleasant land.[13]

Before we leave Isaiah, it is good to widen the scope of his prayer to apply to different nations. We can do this if we have first understood the primary application to Israel. In recent years, we have seen a growing emphasis on the nations, with burdened hearts crying out like the psalmist: 'Ask of me and I will make the nations your inheritance' (Ps 2:8). This is perhaps because it is the time for the nations. Philippe Joret, an apostle to France at this time, in his excellent book *Francement* applies Isaiah 62 to his own nation with typical French passion: 'For France's sake I will not keep silent and for my city's sake I will not rest, until her righteousness goes forth like the dawn, and her salvation as a burning torch. The nations shall see your righteousness.'

---

[13] William Blake, 'Jerusalem' from 'Milton' in *Oxford Book of English Mystical Verse* (OUP, 1917).

Quoting John Knox's 'Give me Scotland or I die', Philippe goes on:

> *Can we say 'Give me France or I die'? That is to say, 'I don't have a reason for living that is more important to me than seeing the kingdom of God revealed over the whole of my nation.' Like Simeon, who waited for the consolation of Israel, and who saw the salvation of the Lord, I say I want to see a powerful revival of faith in Christ and love for God fill my nation. Therefore I say, 'Give me my nation or I don't have a reason to live that satisfies me.' I don't merely want to see these things from afar. A fire is burning in me to see my land visited by God. I long to see my country eating of the tree of life which is given for the healing of the nations.*[14]

I am convinced that as he grows in intimacy with God, the intercessor is likely to catch God's heart for the nations. God's purpose in creating the nations, and how we should regard them, could (and should) be the subject of a whole book. But for the purpose of understanding what will happen as we grow in intimacy with God, it is important to give a brief introduction to the subject here.

Some people react surprisingly strongly against the idea of praying for nations. This seems to be for one of two reasons: the first may be a fear of nationalism and jingoism. When involved in launching the 'Intercession France' movement in the past few years, people have sometimes said to me: *'Ne nous parle pas de prier pour la France: ça fait Front National!'* ('Don't tell us to pray for France: it's like the National Front!') People have said the same thing to me in England when I have suggested in prayer meetings using William Blake's hymn

---

[14] Philippe Joret, *Francement: un jour nouveau sur le pays* (Edtns Joret, 2000). The untranslateable *Francement* is a play on words, meaning 'francely', or 'frankishly'.

'Jerusalem', with its challenging words: 'I shall not cease from mental strife, nor shall my sword sleep in my hand, till we have built Jerusalem in England's green and pleasant land.' My own conviction is that this poem is 'prophetic', that is to say it speaks of what those who follow Christ in England should be doing – building Jerusalem (in this context, the church) in a land that has such potential: England!

The second reason for reticence may be because there has been relatively little published from a theological stance yet to justify the idea of praying for the destiny of nations. Prophetic voices, as we shall see, are calling for it, and intercessors are sensing it, but the idea hasn't hit the theological colleges yet, and so the pastors aren't teaching it. Intercessors may catch the deep travail of the Holy Spirit when the idea is mentioned, but they can't explain it. Pastors may think it's a distraction from the main and plain task of making disciples and planting churches. But it is interesting that when Jesus gave his 'Go and make disciples' great commission, he particularly took the trouble to mention the nations (Mt 28:19). Similarly, when Jesus gives his chilling image about the final judgement, he makes it clear that the judgement will be for the nations: 'But when the Son of man shall come in his glory, and all the angels with him, then shall he sit on the throne of his glory and before him shall be gathered all the nations: and he shall separate them one from another, as the shepherd separates the sheep from the goats' (Mt 25:31–32 RSV).

John Piper's book *Let the Nations Be Glad*[15] is subtitled 'The supremacy of God in missions', and he assumes, as I had always done, that this verse is referring to individuals. But is this what the text actually says? Even though salvation is personal, might there not be in the infinite, colourful creativity of God, a purpose for each nation, a plan for each

[15] John Piper, *Let the Nations Be Glad* (Baker Books, 1993).

people, a call on each country? Might there not be choices that a nation can take which will generally incline the hearts of a people to see and follow Christ? And might there also be choices that can be taken which can harden the hearts of whole generations?

We first come across the term 'nation' in the Bible in Genesis 10, after the flood. We read, 'These are the clans of Noah's sons, according to their lines of descent, within their nations. From these the nations spread out over the earth after the flood' (Gen 10:32). To understand the 'birth' of nations, we must understand the issue of sin. In Ezekiel 28 we see the origin of sin when Lucifer sinned by seeking to rival even God, and as a result God literally disowned him. In Genesis 4 we see sin again: for Cain, 'sin is crouching at the door' (v. 7). On that day of the first murder, Cain moved out of the presence of God. From this passage we get an understanding of the nature of sin. It is not an act, but a nature, a brooding presence: 'Sin is crouching at your door; it desires to have you.' It is a scheming, waiting, crouching being. Then Cain kills and the result is: 'Now you are under a curse.' It is not that God has cursed him, but he is cursed. The results of this calamity grow until in the time of Noah when the thoughts of men's hearts were 'only evil all the time'. The catastrophic flood comes, and after the flood Noah comes out and makes a sacrifice. Then God declares a change of approach, saying in effect, 'I am not going to do that again.' Noah's sons are named, and from these sons God now produces nations: 'These are the clans of Noah's sons, according to their lines of descent, within their nations. From these the nations spread out over the earth after the flood' (Gen 10:32).

Even if for centuries this part of biblical teaching has been neglected, the Bible is clear: God is interested in nations. To Abraham he says: 'This is my covenant with you: You will be the father of many nations. No longer will you be called

Abram; your name will be Abraham, for I have made you a father of many nations' (Gen 17:3–6).

After this there is a time when God deals almost exclusively with Israel. She is the apple of his eye. But not only does she represent the purposes of God on earth, we can also say that he treats her as an example of what God wants in all nations. There are also glimpses or key moments when God speaks to different nations individually. We can study this in Isaiah when God gives different prophecies for different nations. For example, read the surprising passage about the prophetic destiny of Egypt, in Isaiah 19:23: 'In that day there will be a highway from Egypt to Assyria. The Assyrians will go to Egypt and the Egyptian to Assyria. The Egyptians and Assyrians will worship together. In that day Israel will be the third, along with Egypt and Assyria, a blessing on the earth. The Lord Almighty will bless them, saying, "Blessed be Egypt my people, Assyria my handiwork, and Israel my inheritance."'

In Joel we read the following words which some say are being fulfilled today: 'Proclaim this among the nations: Prepare for war! . . . Beat your ploughshares into swords and your pruning hooks into spears. Let the weakling say, "I am strong!" Come quickly, all you nations from every side and assemble there . . . Let the nations be roused; let them advance into the Valley of Jehoshaphat, for there I will sit to judge all the nations on every side . . . Multitudes, multitudes in the valley of decision!' (Joel 3:9–14).

We can think that in the past there was a time when God dealt almost exclusively with Israel. After the day of Pentecost, the non-Jewish people groups did not interest the apostles. It was as if they had to be pushed and prodded to consider them. Then the gospel began to be poured out through Paul, of whom God said, 'This man is a chosen instrument of mine to carry my name before the nations' (Acts 9:15 RSV).

Years later, when Paul preaches in Athens, he seems to have a grasp of the destiny of nations: 'From one man he made every nation of men, that they should inhabit the whole earth; and he determined the times set and the exact places where they should live. God did this so that men would seek him and perhaps reach out for him and find him, though he is not far from each one of us' (Acts 17:26–27). Paul is saying that the nations are God's workings. From Noah, God begins to determine the places and the times. So, according to the Bible, your nation is not an accident and it is not at the mercy of man. God has a purpose for your nation – that men might, within it, seek after him.

Deuteronomy says the same thing: 'When the Most High gave the nations their inheritance, when he divided all mankind, he set up boundaries for the peoples' (Deut 32: 8). This fact – that the nations are the works of God – remains true, even though sometimes in the last centuries their boundaries have been fixed by men in an apparently arbitrary way.[16] It may help us to understand that some conflicts may indeed result from unrighteous decisions made at the time of these boundary changes. On the other hand, in the economy of God, sometimes these changes can work together for good. From looking at nations in general, we could go further and say that through the Old Testament God dealt with the nation of Israel as an example of how he would deal with the nations. Israel is called a 'banner to the nations' (Is 11:10 RSV). Then, for 2000 years, Israel was banned from her land. Since the Second World War, Israel has been created again. Only God could have done this. The fact that Israel has become visible again as a nation may mean, among other things that we will examine in a following chapter, that God is saying: 'Now is the time for the nations.'

---

[16] See Thomas Pakenhams, *The Scramble for Africa 1876–1912* (Weidenfeld and Nicholson, 1991).

This seems like a new emphasis but it is not a completely new idea. In the days after the church Fathers, when missionaries went to new fields, it was with the idea that the whole nation should come to Christ. In times of revival, preachers have sometimes been burdened for their land in a way that has gone beyond their local area, and there have been times of great unity between churches. The destiny of nations has been affected, as happened in England in the eighteenth century. However, these times have been short-lived, and it is fair to say that the revivals turned into denominations. The eighteenth-century revival became Methodism, at least in England; the outpouring at Azusa Street, Los Angeles, in 1905 became the Pentecostal denomination. It is hard to imagine it any differently. But now, in our post-denominational age, in a day of great prayer outpouring, a day of hope of a great end-time harvest, this thought comes back – the idea that a whole nation can be called by God to repentance and to his original purpose. With this comes the idea of making it part of our spiritual discipline of intimacy to pray for the nations with renewed faith and passion.

How to pray for nations

Remitting the sins of a nation and praying for forgiveness

The sins of the past can affect the present. We have mentioned above the phrase 'identificational repentance'. As we draw near to God and are faced with his holiness, it is likely we will begin to confess sin – not just our own sin but the sin of our nation and the sins of our fathers. When Nehemiah heard of the broken-down state of Jerusalem, his reaction was to weep and fast and to confess the sins of his fathers as if they were his own (Neh 1:6).

But can the sins of former generations affect our nation in the present? Absolutely, according to the Bible. There is the incident when King David, whose land is afflicted by famine, enquires of the Lord why this is and is told that it is because the house of Saul has put to death the Gibeonites, a tribe which Joshua swore to protect 300 years earlier (2 Sam 21:1). Even though Saul had died long before and David himself had had nothing to do with this incident, he felt the need to make expiation. It was only when this was settled that blessing came back on the country. It is of utmost importance to say that under the new covenant, of course, the means of expiation is to plead the efficacy of the sacrifice of Christ once and for all for our sins.

This is a mysterious subject, but it is true that many think that the sins of the fathers are being visited on their children in the nations today. The intercessors and the praying church will need to listen to God about these things and be open to 'standing in the gap'. Ezekiel says that God 'looked for a man among them who would build up the wall and stand before me in the gap on behalf of the land so that I would not have to destroy it, but I found none' (Ezek 22:30). God is a God of mercy and he looks for a way of sparing a nation from his just judgement. It seems God seeks intercessors who will confess the sins of the nation. Sin creates a gap in the wall of protection that God places around a nation (see Job 1:10; Ps 34:7). Because of this gap, trouble can enter. Traditionally, it has been thought that intercessors can 'stand in the gap' with their intercession, and particularly through confession of the sins of a nation.

Praying for the 'redemptive purpose'

As an intercessor, praying for your nation may mean not so much praying against the things that are wrong in your nation, but praying into existence the original purpose of God for your nation. It may mean discovering the works prepared in advance for a particular nation to walk in.

In this context, those who are intimate with God may find themselves falling in love with the particular characteristics with which he has gifted different nations and people groups. Often these gifts have been perverted by the devil. The classic example – for a city rather than a nation – is that of Los Angeles. This is the 'City of the Angels', the city of the messengers from God. How that message has been perverted today, with LA as the centre of the film and TV industry carrying messages which are often opposed to God and his values.

As regards France, where I used to live, one national characteristic which is God-given is that of passion. The French are a passionate people and they can be passionate about God. Their worship of him is beautiful, moving, strong and deep. However, I know from living there for ten years that Paris has in places become like a prostitute. Instead of giving a model to the world of passionate intimacy with God, it gives a message of seduction and perversion. The presence of the seats of power of the fashion and cosmetics industry doesn't help. Walking through the city is like walking through one vast pornographic dictionary. What God intended for good the enemy has perverted for bad and the city seems to have cast off all restraint.

The intercessor is calling out to God to 'give him the nation'. He will be praying that the nation will 'feel after God and perhaps find him'. I think he will be praying that the gifts God has given to a nation will be restored. He will be thanking God for the precious things he has put in a nation, for the richness and variety of creation, and praying for the nation to rise from the dead – a bit like Jairus' daughter, the little girl whom Jesus called from the grave back into the purpose for which God had created her.

We have talked of the French, the English and the Californians, but what of the Swiss, with their exemplary thoroughness and depth; the Ugandans with their perseverance through suffering, their intelligence, and their gift of hospitality? What of the fighting gift in prayer that seems to have been placed particularly in Africa, for which I am so grateful and which I covet? What about the Asians and their tears and laughter? What of the Brazilian troubadours of the king with their creativity and stories? What of the Arabs with their gentle-giant streak and their gift of creating community? Let us discover again the different national callings and love them and pray them into being. What an antidote to racism and xenophobia! Let us create, wherever possible, multicultural communities which respect and reflect these gifts and seek to draw them out. Our church in Paris one Pentecost Sunday morning counted no fewer than thirty-three different nations in a congregation of about 350, each with its own gift to bring to the altar of worship. What a foretaste of heaven!

With a whip of rope Jesus cleared out his temple and said that his house would be a house of prayer for . . . whom? Individuals? Families? Sons and daughters? No! It was to be a house of prayer for all nations. Let us understand and take seriously what he meant. I believe that his house will be a place where all nationalities can find God. I believe it is to be a place where we will pray for the nations, that many in each would be saved. It is to be a community which prays for the revealing of the redemptive character in each nation, that God's plan in creating it may be seen.

Praying for a nation's prophetic destiny to be fulfilled

The church is also to be a place where we discover not only the character of God for our country, but his purpose for us at each time of history. We have reproduced in Appendix 2 some prophetic statements which give examples of this for Britain. One nation that has experienced transformation through prayer is Uganda. Not so many years ago, through the oppressive regimes of Idi Amin and the second presidency of Milton Obote, which many Ugandans say was worse, Uganda underwent a terrible time of suffering. It was a period of great danger for Christians as Amin particularly urged the nation to abandon Christianity, and many churches were burned. The woods between Kampala and Jinga became known as the killing fields, and terrible raping of women and murder of children occurred. Often the church was on the run, hiding in the bush, and it was there that Uganda's Christians learnt to pray. They learnt the deep travailing prayer of intercession that the Spirit will bring at such times. They groaned before God as in the pains of childbirth and gradually he heard them. Under Obote the prayer movement continued, giving place in the end to the current regime of President Museveni. After the two dictatorships an equally violent plague hit the country, that of AIDS, and Uganda's problem seemed to be among the worst in Africa.

But Uganda has experienced for several years now a prayer revival so that many of these problems have been turned around. There has been particular, targeted prayer for the nation. There has been fervent prayer planted in every town and district. There have been public prayer meetings in the presence of the President. During one of these he symbolically handed back the Ugandan flag into the hands of the Ugandan intercessors. That which under Amin had at different times been dedicated to witchcraft or Islam, was now being dedicated to Christ. And on New Year's Eve for the Millennium, the President spent the night in the company of tens of thousands of Christians in Kampala football stadium, as the country was dedicated to Jesus Christ at the start of the new century at an all-night prayer gathering. The results of all this are at present impressive. There has been a fall in the rate of AIDS in Uganda, and a dramatic increase in primary school education. There has been a dramatic decrease in corruption and a ten-fold rise in the number of Christian members of parliament. These stories are told in the video *Transformations 2*, among other places, which has some testimony from politicians and leaders and also to certain healings from HIV.[17] For a powerful account of a visit to Kampala's Prayer Mountain, see Appendix 1.The country is still very fragile, but it is demonstrating the words of Isaiah 62 about being available to be watchmen on the walls, being intimate with God to understand what is his burden, and being disciplined enough to give themselves no rest, and to give him no rest, until he has mercy and the land is healed.

---

[17] For a fuller treatment of these stories and some extraordinary testimonies to healings from HIV see the videos *Transformations 2: The Glory Spreads* and *Hope for Uganda* published by The Sentinel Group.

PAUL: CAUGHT UP INTO HEAVEN WITH HIS FEET ON THE GROUND

I have not stopped giving thanks for you, remembering you in my prayers. I keep asking that the God of our Lord Jesus Christ, the glorious Father, may give you the Spirit of wisdom and revelation, so that you may know him better. (Eph 1:16–17)

For this reason I kneel before the Father, from whom his whole family in heaven and on earth derives its name. I pray that out of his glorious riches he may strengthen you with power through his Spirit in your inner being, so that Christ may dwell in your hearts through faith. And I pray that you, being rooted and established in love, may have power, together with all the saints, to grasp how wise and long and high and deep is the love of Christ, and to know this love that surpasses knowledge – that you may be filled to the measure of all the fulness of God.

Now to him who is able to do immeasurably more than all we ask or imagine, according to his power that is at work within us, to him be glory in the church and in Christ Jesus throughout all generations, for ever and ever! Amen. (Eph 3:14–21)

Finally, be strong in the Lord and in his mighty power. Put on the full armour of God so that you can take your stand against the devil's schemes. For our struggle is not against flesh and blood, but against the rulers, against the authorities, against the powers of this dark world and against the spiritual forces of evil in the heavenly realms. Therefore put on the full armour of God, so that when the day of evil comes, you may be able to stand your ground, and after you have done everything, to stand. Stand firm then, with the belt of truth buckled round your waist, with the breastplate of righteousness in place, and with your feet fitted with the readiness that comes from the gospel of peace. In addition to all this, take up the shield of faith, with which you can extinguish all the flaming arrows of the evil one. Take the helmet of salvation and the sword of the Spirit, which is the word of God. And pray in the Spirit on all occasions with all kinds of prayers and requests. With this in mind, be alert and always keep on praying for all the saints.

Pray also for me, that whenever I open my mouth, words may be given me so that I will fearlessly make known the mystery of the gospel, for which I am an ambassador in chains. Pray that I may declare it fearlessly, as I should. (Eph 6:10–20)

We know that the whole creation has been groaning as in the pains of childbirth right up to the present time. Not only so, but we ourselves, who have the firstfruits of the Spirit, groan inwardly as we wait eagerly for our adoption as sons, the redemption of our bodies. For in this hope we were saved. But hope that is seen is no hope at all. Who hopes for what he already has? But if we hope for what we do not yet have, we wait for it patiently.

In the same way, the Spirit helps us in our weakness. We do not know what we ought to pray, but the Spirit himself intercedes for us with groans that words cannot express. And he who searches our hearts knows the mind of the Spirit, because the Spirit intercedes for the saints in accordance with God's will. (Rom 8:22–27)

11

Praying for the Church

> *'I'm a labouring man, and I know but little,*
> *Or nothing at all,*
> *But I can't help feeling that stone once echoed*
> *The voice of Paul.'*
>
> (Thomas Hardy)[1]

The prayer life of Paul is a rich vein of teaching for all those who want to go deeper with God. Paul, with startling confidence, said: 'Be imitators of me, as I am of Christ' (1 Cor 11:1 NASB). Let us see what there is to imitate.

Paul's teaching on the armour of God in Ephesians 6 quoted in full above can have many applications as we fight the good fight of faith; but as we prepare to enter into a deeper intimacy with God, I believe these verses give us helpful steps to enter the place of prayer. First, Paul takes the 'belt of truth'. We can talk to God, thanking him for the truth of the fact that he hears prayer, that he has appointed prayer as a privileged way of being in communion with him. We can edify ourselves and build up our faith by remembering the truth that when we pray, he invites us into a secret place to speak to our Father who is unseen,

[1] Thomas Hardy, 'In the British Museum'.

and that he who 'sees what is done in secret will reward you' (Mt 6:6).

Second, taking the 'breastplate of righteousness', we can thank him that we come in his righteousness, and not through our own. We can delight in recalling the merits of Christ, who became for us 'our righteousness, holiness and redemption' (1 Cor 1:30). Through this we are armoured, and our hearts which are covered by this breastplate are warmed and encouraged to overflow in thankfulness.

Third, the 'shoes of the gospel of peace' help us to walk right into a place of peace with God. These shoes which help us to bring the gospel to others also help us to climb into the heavenly places where we are seated with God in Christ. We have peace with God because of the good news. This is something to ponder and to pray through daily. It is a step toward the throne, to know this 'shalom', well-being, amazing grace, healing for anxious hearts that peace with God and an end to enmity brings. It is a platform of confidence for those who would pray. And we do well to imitate Paul and stand in these shoes of peace.

Fourth, the 'shield of faith' can be lifted up at this time against what Paul calls the 'flaming arrows of the evil one'. These arrows shot at the man or woman who would pray can be thoughts of unbelief that God does not listen. The evil one apparently is the 'accuser' and he may accuse us that there is no point in praying since God does not hear. We need to almost physically 'lift the shield of faith' and say to God that we do believe. We need to exercise faith, to flex the muscles of faith. On a more banal note, the flaming arrows may, I suppose, be the distractions that rush in as soon as the serious Christian decides to pray. His telephone will ring even in the middle of a field; his palm pilot will beep him with a reminder; his spouse will 'just need to reach a decision about this or that'. We need to lift a shield of faith by separating ourselves from distractions to meet with God.

Fifth, the 'helmet of salvation' which covers our heads and therefore our thinking is a reminder that we need to 'put on' the thinking of a child of God. We are sons and daughters and therefore inheritors. We can think as adopted, chosen children who are 'safe' with our Father who sees in secret. We can ask God for our minds to be renewed and transformed so as to understand the will of God, and so as to understand how to pray in the Spirit and according to his will.

As we take up the sixth and last piece of armour which is the 'sword of the Spirit . . .the word of God', we can discover a new and fruitful discipline. Among other things this means we can pray the words of the Bible. As we do, it is as if we wield a powerful weapon. Many Christians are unaware of the weapons at their disposal and remain ineffective. Using the word of God in prayer is a great privilege. It is not just quoting Bible verses at God to make ourselves feel better; but it is 'arming ourselves' with words that reflect the will of God, and hence have authority. In a church prayer meeting it is a good exercise to have all those present praise God using only words from the Bible, or thoughts emanating from or expanding what has just been read. This can increase the vocabulary of prayer of many Christians. I have known times of trial where I have found great safety in praying out loud the words of the psalms. I have found in them all that I needed or wanted to say, as well as many affirming promises. Try for example Psalm 130, which the Book of Common Prayer calls '*de profundis*':

'Out of the depths I cry to you O Lord;
O Lord hear my voice
Let your ears be attentive to my cry for mercy . . .
I wait for the Lord, my soul waits,
And in his word I put my hope . . .
O Israel put your hope in the Lord,
For with the Lord there is unfailing love

And with him is full redemption
He himself will redeem Israel from all their sins.'

As we pray 'O Israel', we are among other things exhorting ourselves. The Spirit is speaking to our spirit, and we are in the presence of the consoling Christ.

I recommend the above 'steps to the throne' as one of the ways to begin a time of prayer. I encourage you to try them.

Paul then finishes this section with the words: 'Pray in the Spirit on all occasions with all kinds of prayers and requests.' Having entered the presence of God let us see what Paul's 'discipline of intimacy' means in practice.

Praying in the Spirit

This could mean praying 'as led by the Spirit', or it could mean praying in tongues. Paul said 'I will pray with my spirit, but I will also pray with my mind' (1 Cor 14:15). And he thanked God that he spoke in tongues more than any of the Corinthians, though in public he preferred prophecy. Praying in tongues can enhance and expand our capacity to pray like nothing else. It is not to be despised. Paul tells us that this gift edifies us (v. 4); it helps us to speak to God (v. 2); and he implies that it is a weapon against the enemy. Some people have extraordinary testimony of the fruit of disciplined tongue-speaking. Jackie Pullinger's story of her breakthrough in the forbidden city of Hong Kong is worth noting. It was as she gave herself daily to regular, disciplined speaking in tongues as part of her prayer time, that extraordinary meetings took place and drug addicts began to be delivered and healed. She was later decorated by the British Government for her work.[2] It should be said, however, that this is not a prescriptive formula. The Holy

[2] Jackie Pullinger, *Chasing the Dragon* (Hodder & Stoughton, 2001).

Spirit alone gives the enabling and energy to maintain a deeper life of intercession. Without him we will simply dry up, so we need to 'pray in the Spirit'. Paul says in Romans 8 that we do not know how to pray as we ought, but the Spirit helps us and intercedes for us with groans too deep for words. It is as if we are joined to Christ and become part of his body, joined to the spirit of prayer in sending prayer up to God. This is a mystery, but those who have an experience of being filled or drenched with the Holy Spirit often testify to an increase in the 'burden', the capacity and the energy to pray as God pours out 'a spirit of grace and supplication' (Zech 12:10).

Praying on all occasions

Paul had learnt the discipline of intimacy. So often when the going is really tough we stop praying, and when it is too easy we stop too. Paul even says he was given a 'thorn in the flesh' which seems to have kept him before God (2 Cor 12:7–10). The occasions of greatest difficulty became the occasions of greatest prayer. For years my reaction to trouble was not necessarily to pray. Instead I would worry, discuss endlessly, get depressed – but I did not spread out my burdens before God. It has only been in recent years, as I have seen the irrefutable fact that prayer is the key to everything and that our God is a God who answers prayer, that it has become my reflex action. But for Paul, it was his discipline in all circumstances to pray. So it was that when they were arrested, Paul and Silas prayed by singing hymns and refused to sit down under the circumstances.

Praying always

Paul writes to the Thessalonians: 'We always thank God for all of you, mentioning you in our prayers' (1 Thess 1:2). And to the Philippians he writes, 'I thank my God every time I remember you. In all my prayers for all of you, I always pray with joy' (Phil 1:3). This is a glimpse into Paul's disciplined prayer life. He cared for his churches like a father. And a father will cry out to God for his own children constantly, if he is wise, so Paul cries out for these churches. He is aware of the constant presence of God and so he is constantly praying.

With all kinds of prayers

Paul had many different ways of talking to God. Just as we can communicate in many different ways with our friends – by letter, telephone, email, face to face, in poetry or song – so Paul describes a variety of expressions to God.

With groaning

In Romans 8:22, Paul speaks of the whole creation 'groaning as in the pains of childbirth', and then goes on to link this specifically to prayer and the work of the Spirit in interceding for us with 'groans that words cannot express'.

Writing to the Corinthians, he again speaks of groaning: 'Meanwhile we groan, longing to be clothed with our heavenly dwelling . . . God has given us the Spirit as a deposit, guaranteeing what is to come' (2 Cor 5:2, 5). Catholic theologian Peter Hocken sees this as a reference to prayer.[3] Having been a student of outpourings of the Holy Spirit, he makes a clear link between these passages and the groaning, 'birthing' prayer which is sometimes to be seen in the current prayer movement. He believes this is to do with anticipating and longing for the kingdom of God.

With weeping

Paul, like Hannah, Joel, Nehemiah and Jesus, knew what it was to weep before God in prayer, in private and also in

[3] Peter Hocken, *The Glory and the Shame* (Eagle, 1994).

public. In his farewell to the Ephesian elders he speaks of serving the Lord 'with great humility and with tears . . . Remember that for three years I never stopped warning each of you night and day with tears' (Acts 20:19, 31). And to the Corinthians he writes: 'For I wrote to you out of great distress and anguish of heart and with many tears' (2 Cor 2:4).

With fasting

Like Hannah, Nehemiah, Joel and Jesus, Paul fasted. No doubt for him, as for Jesus, fasting was not an optional extra. As we have said, fasting is often the master key to unlock doors which otherwise remain shut. And God is at present bringing this discipline back to the church and giving special enabling to do it. He woos us and then draws us out to do it, and then can give us the strength to carry on fasting, giving energy where normally we would give up. Paul's practice was to fast at vital moments of decision in the church. For example, in Acts 13:2: 'While they were worshipping the Lord and fasting, the Holy Spirit said, "Set apart for me Barnabas and Saul for the work to which I have called them."' Then also he was wont to fast at times of commissioning, as in the above incident we read: 'So after they had fasted and prayed, they placed their hands on them and sent them off.' Later, when Paul is founding churches, we read: 'Paul and Barnabas appointed elders for them in each church and, with prayer and fasting, committed them to the Lord in whom they had put their trust' (Acts 14:23).

With a secret history of knowing the glory of the heavenly realms

As for Hannah, Isaiah, Jesus and Daniel, Paul knew what it was to be caught up into the third heaven and hear inexpressible things. This insight into Paul's prayer life is fascinating: 'I know a man in Christ who fourteen years ago was caught up to the third heaven. Whether it was in the body or out of the body I do not know – God knows. And I know that this man – whether in the body or apart from the body I do not know, but God knows – was caught up to Paradise. He heard inexpressible things that man is not permitted to tell. I will boast about a man like that, but I will not boast about myself, except about my weaknesses' (2 Cor 12:2–5). Paul is another intercessor who sees heaven open. Not only on the day of his conversion, where the heavens opened to convict him and even blind him physically, but also on this and perhaps other occasions. Paul had what we have called a 'secret history' to which he seldom referred publicly but which shaped his ministry. He urged the Ephesians to know that they were 'seated in the heavenly places', but notice his discretion: he speaks of 'things that man is not permitted to tell' that he heard while 'caught up into Paradise'.

It's in this passage that Paul also speaks of receiving his 'thorn in the flesh' – 'To keep me from becoming conceited because of these . . . revelations' (v. 7). Such sensitivity often goes with the territory of prophetic intercession.

With persistence in the face of unanswered prayer

Paul shares his experience of prayers that have not been answered. On three different occasions he went to God about his 'thorn'. (An illness? Epilepsy? A frustration in leadership? An unhappy marriage? There are over 350 suggestions as to possible interpretations.[4]) Even though Paul prayed, however, it was not removed. Many reading this will have prayed and prayed in similar situations, but not had their 'thorn' removed. The subject is so important that we will

---

[4] For a full treatment see R.T. Kendall's excellent *The Thorn in the Flesh* (Hodder & Stoughton, 1999).

devote the next chapter to it. But here, Paul's example is deeply encouraging for those struggling. He 'hears' the voice of the Lord saying, 'My grace is sufficient for you, for my power is made perfect in weakness' (v. 9). It is true that sometimes the fact of someone receiving comfort from the grace of God, and the glory shining through their vase of clay, is a more powerful witness than the answered prayer itself. If you are perplexed that your thorn is not removed, take time now to be encouraged, and to let the glory shine through. Comfort others with the comfort you yourself receive from God (2 Cor 1:3–4).

With all kinds of requests

Paul prayed for Israel

'Brothers, my heart's desire and prayer to God for the Israelites is that they may be saved' (Rom 10:1). 'I have great sorrow and unceasing anguish in my heart . . . for the sake of my brothers, those of my own race' (Rom 9:2). We have already looked into this subject, which is increasingly gripping the church, but here is another reminder not to miss this element in the prayer life of Paul, lest we fail to understand his balanced example.

Paul prayed for the government

In his letter to Timothy, he writes the lines which have had a great influence on anointed liturgies like the 1662 Prayer Book: 'I urge then, first of all, that requests, prayers, intercession and thanksgiving be made for everyone – for kings and all those in authority, that we may live peaceful and quiet lives . . . I want men everywhere to lift up holy hands in prayer' (1 Tim 2:1–2, 8). It is a good discipline to be informed about those in authority and have their names readily to hand. Keep a list of the members of the government and those in authority in the education and media, and pray for them that in a time of peace the gospel may advance.

Paul prayed for the church

It is clear that this was the main focus of Paul's prayer, and we might say his main burden. He was certainly the church-planting apostle to the Gentiles. It is important to see that New Testament prayers were not really that the unconverted would be saved, but rather that Christians would be so filled with a vision of heaven and with the fire of God that they would have the courage to be witnesses – literally, be martyrs – to Jesus with signs and wonders following. Paul's prayers for the churches had a three-fold focus:

1. He prayed that they would be bold. This to Paul is more important than insignificant circumstances like being released from prison! It still takes my breath away to read of Paul saying to the Colossians, 'And pray for us, too, that God may open a door for our message, so that we may proclaim the mystery of Christ, for which I am in chains' (Col 4:3). He wrote to the Ephesians, asking for prayer to preach the gospel 'for which I am an ambassador in chains. Pray that I may declare it fearlessly, as I should' (Eph 6:20). His dedication humbles us, although there are apostolic preachers today, like Denis Balcombe in China, who have often been in prison because of their preaching. Let us regain the primacy of announcing Christ wherever we are, before rich or poor, before the weak and the powerful alike. Let us tirelessly make this a subject for our prayer. So focused was Paul on praying in this way, that when he was before Festus, he refused to be released, preferring to appeal to Caesar and thus get to preach the gospel in Rome, even though in chains. He pleaded the case of Christ with Festus and King Agrippa; not asking to be released from his chains, but that 'not only you but all who are listening to me today may become what I am, except for these chains' (Acts 26:29).

2. He prayed that they would be filled with wisdom and understanding. Paul prays some deep prayers of rich content which we do well to copy into our prayer journals and learn by heart, that we might pray them for those who need our prayers. He writes to the Ephesians, for example: 'I have not stopped giving thanks for you, remembering you in my prayers. I keep asking that the God of our Lord Jesus Christ, the glorious Father, may give you the Spirit of wisdom and revelation, so that you may know him better' (Eph 1:17). This prayer for revelation is so important; from our vision of Christ and his love all our ministry can flow. What else does this prayer ask for? It asks that we might:

- have a spirit of wisdom;
- be given revelation so that we would know him better;
- know the riches of our inheritance;
- know his incomparably great power;
- know the mighty strength of his resurrection;
- know Christ's position, far above all authorities;
- know his headship over everything for the church, his body;
- know the fullness of him who fills everything!

3. He prayed that they would have a love affair with the church. I have fallen in love three times in my life. I'll never forget the third time. It was in the city of York in the 1970s. I was 26 years old. She was beautiful and classy. There was a perfume about her. I was moved by how she loved people and served them. She knew all about the arts, both historical and contemporary. She had a beautiful voice and her music made me cry. She was gorgeous! I'm talking about the church. I first came across her under David Watson's leadership in York. I had never seen anything like it in my life. People were living in community, the poor were being helped, artistic gifts were coming to life, the worship was out of this world, the aroma of love was there. It was the church, just as Jesus intended her! A short time later I gave up my job and decided to devote the rest of my life to building such communities.

The second time I fell in love was when I encountered Christ in all his majesty. See the last chapter of this book for more about that love affair which grows even in times of sorrow.

But the first time I fell in love was with the person who later became my wife. From the moment she slipped her arm in mine in Christ Church Meadow on the university campus in Oxford, I knew I was sunk. My stomach churned slightly and my heart stopped briefly. I was in love! Since then I have not stopped learning new things about Anita, the bride of my youth. She is still the most beautiful and fascinating person I know and constantly surprises me. I will never come to the end of getting to know her.

But it is the same with the church, the bride of Christ. I feel I have only just begun to love her and know her. I think it is legitimate to talk of loving the church even though we are part of her, because Christ loves her and we are called to love the things he loves. When I moved to France and discovered the Church for all Nations, it was a big new discovery. A church on earth, with thirty nations living in harmony, is a prophetic foretaste of heaven, where every nation and tribe and tongue will worship God. I discovered the church among the poor and serving the poor. I have loved her even more fiercely since.

Graham Cray says: 'We are in a culture which is not so much secular, sceptical and rationalistic, as religiously plural and relativist.'[5] He goes on: 'Spiritual experience is back in the public square, but any and every religious experience, for

---

[5] Graham Cray, *John Wimber: His Influence and Legacy* (Eagle, 1998).

there are no longer any universally accepted maps of the territory. Churches which are rationalistic and sceptical of the supernatural will drive seekers into the arms of any numbers of cults and new age groups. What we need are culturally accessible churches with a Christ-centred supernaturalism.'

Paul had this passion for a church that could reach the lost, a church that was growing and growing. And we have to understand that passion in order to understand his prayer life. Paul is striving for the church when he writes to the Colossians: 'I rejoice in what was suffered for you . . . for the sake of his body, which is the church. I have become its servant by the commission God gave me to present the word of God to you in its fulness . . . To this end I labour, struggling with all his energy, which so powerfully works in me' (Col 1:24–25, 29).

Paul says he labours and strives for the church. He does not cease to make mention of her in his prayers. He prays that she may be full of the glory of God. To the Ephesians he writes: 'To him be glory in the church and in Christ Jesus throughout all generations, for ever and ever!' And when writing to the Romans, of course, he says: 'I make much of my ministry in the hope that I may somehow arouse my own people to envy and save some of them' (Rom 11:14).

So we see that Paul's prayer burden and his practice of prayer were strong but perfectly balanced, with rich food for meditation and imitation. And now we turn to the master prayer warrior, the Lord Jesus, as we conclude our examination of intercessors practising the discipline of an intimate walk with the Father.

SEVEN BURDENS OF CHRIST

I pray for them. I am not praying for the world, but for those you have given me, for they are yours. All I have is yours, and all you have is mine. And glory has come to me through them. I will remain in the world no longer, but they are still in the world, and I am coming to you. Holy Father, protect them by the power of your name – the name you gave me – so that they may be one as we are one. While I was with them, I protected them and kept them safe by that name you gave me. None has been lost except the one doomed to destruction so that Scripture would be fulfilled.

I am coming to you now, but I say these things while I am still in the world, so that they may have the full measure of my joy within them. I have given them your word and the world has hated them, for they are not of the world any more than I am of the world. My prayer is not that you take them out of the world but that you protect them from the evil one. They are not of the world, even as I am not of it. Sanctify them by the truth; your word is truth. As you sent me into the world, I have sent them into the world. For them I sanctify myself, that they too may be truly sanctified.

My prayer is not for them alone. I pray also for those who will believe in me through their message, that all of them may be one, Father, just as you are in me and I am in you. May they also be in us so that the world may believe that you have sent me. I have given them the glory that you gave me, that they may be one as we are one: I in them and you in me. May they be brought to complete unity to let the world know that you sent me and have loved them even as you have loved me.

Father, I want those you have given me to be with me where I am, and to see my glory, the glory you have given me because you loved me before the creation of the world.

Righteous Father, though the world does not know you, I know you, and they know that you have sent me. I have made you known to them, and will continue to make you known in order that the love you have for me may be in them and that I myself may be in them. (Jn 17:9–25)

Then Jesus went with his disciples to a place called Gethsemane, and he said to them, 'Sit here while I go over there and pray.' He took Peter and the two sons of Zebedee along with him, and he began to be sorrowful and troubled. Then he said to them, 'My soul is overwhelmed with sorrow to the point of death. Stay here and keep watch with me.'

Going a little farther, he fell with his face to the ground and prayed, 'My Father, if it is possible, may this cup be taken from me. Yet not as I will, but as you will.'

Then he returned to his disciples and found them sleeping. 'Could you men not keep watch with me for one hour?' he asked Peter. 'Watch and pray so that you will not fall into temptation. The spirit is willing, but the body is weak.'

He went away a second time and prayed, 'My Father, if it is not possible for this cup to be taken away unless I drink it, may your will be done.' (Mt 26:36–42)

It was now about the sixth hour, and darkness came over the whole land until the ninth hour, for the sun stopped shining. And the curtain of the temple was torn in two. Jesus called out with a loud voice, 'Father, into your hands I commit my spirit.' When he had said this, he breathed his last. (Lk 23:44–46)

12

Seven Prayer Burdens of Christ

'To heaven their prayers
Flew up, nor missed the way, by envious winds
Blown vagabond or frustrate: in they passed,
Dimensionless through Heavenly doors; then clad
With incense, where the golden altar fumed,
By their great intercessor, came in sight
Before the Father's throne: them the glad Son
Presenting, thus to intercede began.'

(John Milton)[1]

'The fact that Christ and we become one, means that what applies to Christ applies to us, and that we can in a way unknown to the rest of the world, call God our Father, no longer by analogy, no longer in terms of anticipation or prophecy, but in terms of Christ. This has a direct bearing on . . . prayer.'

(Metropolitan Anthony)[2]

---

[1] John Milton, *Paradise Lost*, Book XI ll 15–21.
[2] Anthony Bloom, *Living Prayer* (Darton, Longman & Todd, 1999) p. 56.

The disciples came to Jesus and said, 'Teach us to pray.' What a wonderful gift it is that we can be 'with Christ in the school of prayer'.[3] And how we need his help for this discipline!

When we look at Jesus' prayer life, we are struck by its constancy and its naturalness, but also by its discipline. By this I mean he clearly lived in the presence of his Father, he was always attentive to his voice. Particularly in John's gospel we see Jesus speaking of his constant communication with his Father. But at the same time, there are times of daily discipline, times of deep communication, and times of passion and intensity. Such is the beauty of the Master's life; in all fields he is supreme, and particularly so in this field of prayer.

It is hard to know which came first, the discipline or the 'practising of the presence'. At any rate, we see that Jesus' habit was to get up early. Right at the start of his gospel, even though it is the most compressed of the four, Mark takes the trouble to show us that 'very early in the morning, while it was still dark, Jesus got up, left the house and went off to a solitary place, where he prayed' (Mk 1:35). This happens after the powerful but long evening when, Jesus having healed Peter's mother-in-law, 'the whole town gathered at the door' and they brought to him all who were sick or demonised. Nevertheless, Jesus rose early, knowing his need and his enjoyment of the Father's presence. At this moment it seems Jesus gained insight for the day ahead, for when Simon and the others find him they try to persuade him to come back, but Jesus says no: 'Let us go somewhere else – to the nearby villages – so that I can preach there also. That is why I came.'

Jesus' prayer was not something that kept him from doing courageously the work of the kingdom. On the contrary, it

---

[3] See Andrew Murray, *With Christ in the School of Prayer* (Ambassador Productions, 1998).

led him to the lost. This needs stressing, because some churches that have become involved in the prayer movement have found that after a while fewer people are coming to Christ, fewer of the poor are being helped, and so on. If this is the case, we have to ask if their prayers are really a spirit-led exercise. For the perfect intercessor became the patient evangelist. Loving God will lead to loving the lost, as we have said before; prayer should lead to action.

A second fascinating aspect of Jesus' prayer life is that it was constant. Many incidents in the gospel of John point this out. We glimpse it at the tomb of Lazarus, when he prays out loud for the resurrection of Lazarus but says, 'Father, I thank you that you have heard me. I knew that you always hear me, but I said this for the benefit of the people standing here, that they may believe that you sent me' (Jn 11:41–42). So for Christ, knowing that God heard him always was a fact of life. We see it in the significant discussion with the Pharisees in John 5, after the healing of the man paralysed for thirty-eight years. He says, 'My Father is always at his work to this very day, and I, too, am working.' He then adds, 'I tell you the truth, the Son can do nothing by himself; he can do only what he sees his Father doing, because whatever the Father does, the Son also does. For the Father loves the Son, and shows him all he does' (Jn 5:19–20). This is a privilege to aspire to, the daily walking with God that Jesus exhibits. It is certainly the goal of the discipline of intimacy. The lessons learnt early, morning by morning, lead to the ability to listen moment by moment to the Father.

A third aspect of Jesus' praying is that he shows at times that intensity and passion that we have seen in all the intercessors we have mentioned. Jesus talks of always praying and not giving up, and of 'his chosen ones who cry out to him day and night' (Lk 18:1, 7). He himself is described by the writer to the Hebrews as 'offering up prayers and petitions with loud cries and tears to the one who could save him from death, and he was heard because of his reverent submission' (Heb 4:7). He did this in Gethsemane, too, where 'being in anguish, he prayed more earnestly, and his sweat was like drops of blood' (Lk 22:44). Matthew records that, just before the commissioning of the twelve, Jesus' passionate concern was for the people, 'harassed and helpless, like sheep without a shepherd', which prompts his call to prayer: 'Ask the Lord of the harvest, therefore, to send out workers into his harvest field' (Mt 9:36, 38). And we can feel his burden also in the poignant sigh over Jerusalem – which is like a prophetic prayer: 'O Jerusalem, Jerusalem, you who kill the prophets and stone those sent to you, how often I have longed to gather your children together, as a hen gathers her chicks under her wings, but you were not willing' (Mt 23:37).

Fourthly, Jesus taught the need for humility and reality, rather than 'many words' or self-importance. The parable of the Pharisee and the tax collector reminds us that it is better in the sight of God to confess our uselessness and to ask for mercy, than to be proud of our prayerfulness. The preface to the Lord's prayer encourages us not to pile up empty words but to go to our Father who is in secret. This is salutary, humbling advice to keep before us as we tread into the holy ground of Jesus' prayer to the Father. I believe he carries seven burdens into that place of prayer.

1. Jesus prays for the protection of the saints

We begin with Jesus' fullest and longest recorded prayer – his 'high priestly' prayer in John 17, so called because it shortly precedes his ultimate sacrifice of himself.

> *I pray for them. I am not praying for the world, but for those you have given me . . . protect them by the power of your name – the name you gave me . . . while I was with them, I protected them and kept them safe by the name you gave me.*

None has been lost except the one doomed to destruction so that the Scripture would be fulfilled. I am coming to you now, but I say these things while I am still in the world so that they may have the full measure of my joy within them. I have given them your word and the world has hated them, for they are not of the world any more than I am of the world. My prayer is not that you take them out of the world but that you protect them from the evil one.

Jesus is acutely aware of the battle he is fighting and of the hatred that will be directed against his followers. He shows this concern also when he teaches them to pray, 'Lead us not into temptation and deliver us from the evil one.' We can imitate his prayer: 'Keep them in your name . . . I have guarded them . . . I have given them your word . . . now keep them from the evil one.' When we consider the enemy's assaults against the church, against fruitfulness, against intimacy with God, we can pray this prayer with energy. When we consider the fragility, in some countries, of the next generation of Christian leaders and the forces ranged against them, we will pray this prayer.

According to John Piper 'Probably the number one reason why prayer malfunctions in the hands of believers is that we try to turn a wartime walkie-talkie into a domestic intercom. Until you know that life is war, you cannot know what prayer is for. Prayer is for the accomplishment of a wartime mission.'[4] This perspective helps us to understand Jesus' prayer: 'Protect them from the evil one.' He is praying for his resistance forces against their capture! Piper continues: 'We simply must seek for ourselves and for our people a wartime mentality. Otherwise the biblical teaching about the urgency of prayer, and the vigilance of prayer, and the watching in prayer and the persevering in prayer, and the danger of

[4] John Piper, *Let the Nations Be Glad*, p. 46.

abandoning prayer will make no sense and find no resonance in our hearts.'

2. Jesus prays for the holiness of the saints

'Sanctify them by the truth; your word is truth. As you sent me into the world, I have sent them into the world. For them I sanctify myself, that they too may be truly sanctified' (vv. 17–18).

This is the second burden that we would do well to understand: the holiness of the people of God. It has to do with being set apart, separated, holy, pure, different. It has to do with praying for Christians to leave their comfort zones, to leave the norm of society in order to be sent into the world by Christ. Evidently the Bible, the word of truth, is a vital agent in this process. I believe this is one of the most important themes for the church in Europe. In the capital cities of Europe, the church will find that she is a hospital for hurting casualties. She will be besieged by godless postmodern values. The purity of individual Christians is far from assured and this process of becoming the holy people of God is a vital subject for intercession and exhortation.

In the year 2001 in America a new kind of hero briefly emerged. These were the fire-fighters of New York. On the day of the 11 September attacks on the World Trade Center, it became apparent that acts of great bravery had been committed by the rescue teams. There was the call made by a worker to his wife as he went up the stairs to the top of the building. He said that he might not come out alive, but that he loved her and wanted her to know they had had a good life together. They were the last words she ever heard from him. Then there was the man who was interviewed at 'Ground Zero' after twenty-five hours of constant toil as a rescue worker. His eyes and clothes and mouth were caked in dust and he was asked if he would be taking a rest now.

His reply was memorable: 'How can I rest? As long as there are people buried who are counting on me under there, this is no time for rest.' Here was a group of people who at some point had made a choice to be set apart. It was not in the heat of the moment that they made it, but it was a considered choice. It was accompanied by training, followed by service and, in the end, resulted in sacrifice.

Clearly this can be an example for Christians: we are to be a people who have at some point made a choice; individuals who have decided to be separated for a task. We have asked for and received training. We have dedicated our lives to the task of rescue. And when the day of trouble comes, we will be ready.

One rich theme to meditate on is that of the Nazirites. We find them throughout the Old Testament and into the New – people who from birth or later made the choice. It was a choice for holiness, a choice to come away from the norm, a choice to be set apart. At every point in history, it seems, when God is inaugurating a new era, he calls people apart from their comfort zone to trust in him. Jesus prays for his people to be sanctified, which has to do with separation. Abraham was separated. Joseph was forcibly separated. Moses had to leave the comfort of the court of Pharaoh and go into the desert where he met God. And when he came back he stood not in any confidence gleaned from his education at Pharaoh's court but through his education in the presence of the God of truth. Jesus said, 'Sanctify them by the truth; your word is truth.' We can think of Samuel, set apart from his birth, and we can think of our own children and our godly longings for them, and we can imitate Jesus and pray, 'Sanctify them by your truth.' We can go on to meditate on others, right into the New Testament, where John the Baptist 'goes apart', as does Paul after him, and fulfils a Nazirite vow. Prophetic voices are saying that now is the time for the same separation to God that the Nazirites exhibited.[5] We could even say that this was always God's design for the church, but that we have lost our radicalness; that materialism has strangled our prophetic voice. Pray therefore with Christ that we may be set apart for his truth.

For myself, moving with four growing children from church-rich England to France was a choice of this kind. We moved from a large house to a small apartment, a smaller salary, a smaller church. We moved from the suburbs to the inner city. All our work was to be in a foreign language, so we couldn't even rely on our own eloquence. We had become like babies again. This 'downward mobility' went against the grain. Everything in me was at war with the call of God. But at the same time, we were moving to greater dependency on God, a greater challenge, and greater potential. We were moving into a sharpened arena of training, a situation in which we were 'set apart' from our comfort zone. It was the best move we could have made. I recommend it!

3. Jesus prays for the love and unity of the saints

My prayer is not for them alone. I pray also for those who will believe in me through their message, that all of them may be one, Father, just as you are in me and I am in you. May they also be in us so that the world may believe that you have sent me. I have given them the glory which you gave me, that they may be one as we are one: I in them and you in me. May they be brought to complete unity to let the world know that you sent me and have loved them even as you have loved me.'

'Trinity Unity' is what it has been called,[6] this longing

[5] See Lou Engle, *Digging the Wells of Revival* (Revival Press, 1998), pp. 193–205.

[6] For a full treatment see Joy Dawson, *Intimate Friendship with God* (Kingsway, 2001).

coming from the heart of God. What Jesus prays for is a unity that goes much further than what we may have experienced in the church. He prays, and we can pray, 'that they may be one even as we are one'. That is to say, we can think of the confidence, submission, trust and respect in the relationship between Father, Son and Holy Spirit, and we can aspire to it. The Father and the Son *complete* each other's work, they do not *compete*. You never know when one leaves off and the other begins. In the work of salvation: 'No-one comes to the Father except through me,' says Christ (Jn 14:6). But he also says: 'No-one can come to me unless the Father . . . draws him' (Jn 6:44). Similarly, in our ministry as a church we should complement one another in working for the same goal. Jesus prayed for this and believed it possible; we can believe it for all spheres of the church – between husband and wife, brothers and sisters; between members of a church; between different churches in a town or different denominations in a nation. In this relationship, each glorifies the other. They submit to one another, they love one another. We can repent of divisions, so that the Holy Spirit is not grieved. We can take time and trouble to be with different people or groups of people for the sake of unity, praying the prayer of Jesus all the while.

It is clear to me that no one group of Christians has a monopoly on the truth. To win a town or city we will do well to work in unity and to be seen to work in unity. For ten years I had the privilege of serving a church in France which had a history of persecution of the Protestant church, and what could almost be called a spirit of division upon the evangelical church. In 1572 the River Seine ran red with the blood of the Protestant martyrs as, on St Bartholomew's Day, 10,000 Huguenots were killed in Paris alone. Then when England had a revival in the eighteenth century, France had a bloody revolution. In its turn the Catholic church was persecuted, and the consequences in anti-

Christian thought are still felt in the fiercely secular state which France has become today. And yet there is a passion for God in the country and a commitment to authenticity that anglophones would do well to learn from. In Paris, Anita and I worked for reconciliation and renewal, involving ourselves in gatherings small and large whose goals were repentance, reconciliation and intercession for revival.[7] I have discovered how deep and painful some divisions can be, and also that, if you are prepared to be a bridge, it's inevitable that people will walk over you. Much prayer and friendship is needed. At the same time, we have seen what happens when Catholics and Protestants get together around the person of Christ. It is as if the Holy Spirit is no longer grieved, and the anointing and presence of God can be very real, and healing abounds. So it is that I pray and work for unity, not in an official capacity but in unofficial gatherings that I hope reflect this prayer of Jesus.

Jesus prays for us to be one even as he and the Father are one. We can get into the presence of the Father, we can practise his presence, which has to do with 'being one' in Christ and in the Father. As we experience this, it is likely that a desire for unity and a love for Christians of other confessions will become our priorities and our joy. How are you living this out? The answer to this may depend on the sense of need where we live, and on how much division there is. But in any country, Christians should examine themselves and see whether they are praying and living the prayer of Jesus. Have we 'fallen in love with the whole church' (to use an expression of John Wimber)? And if so, are we taking time to express that love with those who aren't like us, but who love Christ?

It is more an attitude of heart than a use of time, although

[7] Particularly two charities called *Embrase Nos Cœurs* and *Intercession France.*

it will take our time. It will affect the way we speak about others. Joy Dawson used to say that to withhold approval is the same as to criticise. Trinity Unity calls us to 'glorify' other Christians, to be enthusiastic about them, to speak lovingly of them and not to withhold our approval. May we pray and live so that we can be one, as he and the Father are one.

4. Jesus prays for the witness and mission of the saints

'That the world may believe . . . That the world will know that you sent me.' Jesus is praying for the lost. His eyes are on the 'other towns', on the 'other sheep who are not of this sheep pen'. But he knows that there are conditions which favour belief or unbelief, and that we cannot take short cuts around them. Hence loving unity and effective witness are prayed for in the same breath. It is also true that if we are joined to the Godhead and become one in him, then the world will begin to believe. Jesus does not instruct his disciples to pray for particular individuals 'out there' to believe. Rather in another memorable passage on prayer he says: 'The harvest is plentiful but the workers are few. Ask the Lord of the harvest, therefore, to send out workers into his harvest field' (Mt 9:37–38). Here we can learn to understand timing. We can learn about vision and hopefulness and lifting up our heads. But we also learn that Jesus instructs us to make labourers a target for prayer in these days. I believe every pastor who feels alone should begin to pray this specifically. James said we don't have because we don't ask. So let's ask.

To fuel our prayer for labourers, here are two ideas: first, pray for planters of cell groups. One of the emphases the Holy Spirit is giving to the church at present is that of cell-church structure. The church must become small in order to become large. The cells planted are to be places to invite friends and see them come to Christ. 'Every Christian a leader and every home a church' is a motto from the explosive cell-church movement in Columbia. Churches which understand the fruitfulness of the cell-church structure can pray for labourers or leaders. The labourers needed are imitators of Christ who is the Good Shepherd. The Good Shepherd has his eyes looking outward to the other sheep that he must bring also. Every Christian reading this book can make it his goal to ask the Lord of the harvest for labourers in every field of the church, so that the world may believe.

A second idea to apply this prayer to is that of a world vision. This prayer has to do with the nations. For Western Christians, traditionally 'the harvest fields' were the nations, particularly the two-thirds world. Now it seems there is sometimes a greater need in Europe. But wherever our focus, there is still a prayer to pray for missionaries to be sent out to harvest fields that are not just our own. I believe that it is one of the callings of Britain to serve other nations and to be a source of blessing. Let's remember men like William Carey and 'Praying Hyde', who both served in India; Henry Martyn who left Cambridge for India and then went to Iran and the Muslim world; William Burns (called 'Greatheart'), Hudson Taylor in China, and C.T. Studd in both China and Africa. Of course we need a modern missiological understanding of where to go. Evidently the 10/40 window remains a field of great need, but where few doors are open. Let us gain a yearning for labourers to be sent out into the harvest field, whatever the sacrifice, and let us pray to the Lord of the harvest for this.

The nations to which missionaries went in the past are now sending labourers back to Europe, at least when they can get a visa. This can be a gift to the churches in this 'dark continent'. Pray that the Lord of the harvest will also send labourers back from South America, from Africa, from

China, to evangelise the nations from which their spiritual grandparents came. Pray for organisations like 'Go to the Nations' (Brazil') or 'Trumpet Mission' (Uganda) or 'Revival Church' (China) which have this focus. When people come from outside, provided they properly understand the culture, they can have a faith that rises above the norm in the country which they have now adopted. We can beseech the Lord for this. In our church in Paris we had in our team full-time labourers who were African (Togolese), Swiss, English, Lebanese, Norwegian, American, Brazilian and French all at one time. I thank God for the rich variety of those who hear his call. I thank God that he is sending labourers into the ripe harvest field which is France and I pray he will send them to Britain as well.

5. Jesus prays that his people will see his glory

God is a God of relationship. He loves the world. The whole of the Bible is the story of his longing for his people. Jesus is the fulfilment of several who responded to the call to glory. Enoch was one – it is said he 'walked with God'. Moses was another – he cried out to God, 'Show me your glory!' Here Jesus prays: 'Father, I want those you have given me to be with me where I am, and to see my glory, the glory you have given me because you loved me before the creation of the world.' Jesus evidently longed for his disciples to see the glory that he knew and to understand the love of God as revealed in this glory. These things are mysteries, but there are those who can testify to their apprehension of the glory of God.

I love the testimony of Charles Finney: 'Without expectation of it, without ever having thought in my mind that there was any such thing . . . the Holy Spirit descended on me in a manner that seemed to go through my soul; I could feel the impression, like waves of liquid power going through and through me. Indeed it seemed to come in waves and waves of liquid love, for I could not express it any other way. And yet it did not seem like water but rather the breath of God. I can recollect distinctly that it seemed to fan me, like immense wings, and it seemed to me as these waves passed over me that they literally moved my hair like a passing breeze.'[8] This is the glory about which Christ prays.

Blaise Pascal's *Testament*, sewn into his jacket and discovered ten years after his death by his servant, speaks memorably of it:

> *In the year of grace 1654*
> *From about half past ten in the evening until about half past twelve*
> *FIRE*
> *God of Abraham, God of Isaac, God of Jacob, not of the philosophers and scholars*
> *Certitude. Certitude. Feeling. Joy. Peace.*
> *God of Jesus Christ. . . .*
> *Joy joy joy, tears of joy. . . .*
> *This is eternal life that they might know thee the only true God and the one thou hast sent, Jesus Christ . . . Eternally in Joy for one day's training on earth!*[9]

T. S. Eliot says of Pascal, 'Because of his unique combination and balance of qualities, I know of no religious writer more pertinent to our time.'[10] Pascal was a seventeenth-century French mathematician and philosopher. He

---

[8] In Colin Whittaker, *Seven Great Prayer Warriors* (Marshall Pickering, 1987).

[9] Blaise Pascal, in *Shorter Works of Pascal* (Translation: Westminster, 1948) p. 117.

[10] In his Introduction to the Everyman edtn of Pascal's *Pensées*.

is referring to epiphanic experiences of Abraham, of Isaac and of Jacob and making a link with his own. And I believe this is what Jesus was praying for when he asked that we might 'see his glory'. I believe that we can come back to such experiences of his majesty in the same way that we can come back to our first love. Jesus prays for us to be with him where he is, to see his glory. This has happened in times of revival, as the eighteenth-century accounts of Jonathan Edwards so clearly show. This careful academic, who later became Principal of Yale, wrote this on the subject of seeing the glory: 'It was very wonderful to see how a person's affections were sometimes moved – when God did as it were suddenly open their eyes and let into their minds a sense of the greatness of His grace, the fullness of Christ, and His readiness to save . . . their joyful surprise caused their hearts as it were to leap, so that they have been ready to break forth into laughter, tears often at the same time issuing like a flood, and intermingling with loud weeping . . . The manner of God's working on the soul, sometimes especially, is very mysterious.'[11] So it is that with Christ we can pray that we and that other Christians be with him to see his glory.

6. Jesus prays for abandonment to the Father's will

> *He took Peter and the two sons of Zebedee along with him, and he began to be sorrowful and troubled. Then he said to them, 'My soul is overwhelmed with sorrow to the point of death. Stay here and keep watch with me.' Going a little farther, he fell with his face to the ground and prayed, 'My Father, if it is possible, may this cup be taken from me. Yet not as I will, but as you will' (Mt 26:37–39).*

[11] Quoted in Guy Chevreau, *Catch the Fire* (Marshall Pickering, 1994) p. 93.

We enter now the holy ground of Jesus' last recorded prayers. And our understanding of intimacy with God will be incomplete without this. This is praying in a desperate pass. This is praying and not giving up. This is praying with tears and sorrow when there is a sense of doom and even defeat. This is reaching out to the garment of the Father in the same way that people had reached out to touch the garment of Christ to be set free.

There is a beautiful painting by Delacroix of Christ in the Garden of Gethsemane.[12] He is lying with his arms outstretched, reaching, longing. However, this is Christ praying when there is no answer, when the heavens are silent. It is of course a unique event – the Son of Almighty God is going to his agony and to his end. All his life, he has been walking in this direction – towards separation, towards confrontation with the last enemy, death. It is the moment in which the future of mankind hangs on a hinge. History is turning, and heaven waits in silence.

We are not given to walk such paths, but we are called in our small way to imitate Christ. We are called to moments when our future, or the future of our family, hangs in the balance. We are called to give up our lives. We are called to suffer. We are called to embrace the Father's will, which may not be our own. John White comments: 'One may say we have no right to compare our small dilemmas with His great one. Yet why not? Is not the whole point that He trod the road of deepest perplexity ahead of us. To be sure, we have no Gethsemane, no horror of such blackness. Yet with mingled sorrow and gladness we may watch Him as the disciples sleep, and see that we have a High Priest who can be touched by the feelings of our own weakness. He has passed that way Himself.'[13]

---

[12] 'L'Agonie dans le jardin de Gethsemane', Delacroix, Rijksmuseum, Amsterdam.

[13] John White, *People in Prayer* (IVP, 1977) p. 145.

What can we learn from the Master in this school of prayer? First, we can be comforted by the fact that he expresses his need for fellowship. He asks his close friends to stay there and pray. He wants their agreement and their support. We too can and should express this to our close associates, not hiding our need of them. Sometimes in Paris we had to call on the two pastor couples we were closest to in our church in times of distress, sickness, battle, or when we experienced apparent betrayal. We would do our best to stand together. Interestingly, Jesus' friends on this occasion didn't quite live up to the challenge. And it is true that there may be times when we have to go it alone.

Secondly, we see that real sorrow and real anxiety do not lead him away from his Father, but rather towards him. For many of us it is the opposite: 'I'm so worried I can't pray' is the cry. We can learn to turn our terrors into times with our Father. The psalmist's cry is, 'Out of the depths I cry to you, O Lord.' He is Christ's forerunner in not hesitating to call on God in the time of trouble. And in being real. He teaches us, as does Hannah, to pour out our soul in bitterness towards God.

Next we see the unashamed prayer for a solution – that this cup pass from him. The issue narrows down to one thought. Was there no other way? A way that would avoid the limitless blackness that would engulf him? We see Jesus asking, like Abraham interceding for Sodom. We see dialogue and relationship even in a time of trauma. In the end, he acquiesces. He seems to see by faith that he must tread this path, and he goes back to his disciples. Having spoken to them, he again gets alone with his Father and continues the questioning. In times of trial, we may have experienced this too. At one point there is peace, but it is short-lived. There is a moment of hope and confidence, but then it vanishes. Three times Jesus prays this prayer, until in the end there is a sense of completion, and the decision – 'May your will be done' – holds. This is what it means to be a Christian, and it is well that we rehearse this prayer and settle the answer in every department of our lives, so that when the war intensifies we are able to hold to the direction that God is giving us, and hold on to him.

7. Jesus abandons his spirit into the Father's hands

At the end, Jesus comes to his final prayer: 'Father, into your hands I commit my spirit' (Lk 23:46). He has come through the storms, but he does not die in torment. He dies knowing that 'It is finished'. He dies as he lived, abandoning his life to his Father, entrusting his spirit into his Father's hands. Although the time is unique, the victory is unique and the Son is unique, we can nevertheless learn things for our own relationship with the Father. Jesus goes before us, believing in life after death, and believing in the goodness of his Father. He believes in the Father's ability to take care of his spirit. He is ready to die. This is a rare treasure today, to be at peace at the hour of our death, without fear and ready for our going. And we can learn it from Christ.

We may say that Christianity is for living and not for dying, but if we say this we make a profound mistake. When Zechariah prophesied about his son John, the forerunner of Christ, his prophecy included the promise that the Saviour would 'rescue us from the hand of our enemies, and enable us to serve him without fear'. He goes on to say that the Saviour will 'shine on those living in darkness, and in the shadow of death' (Lk 1:74, 79). This prayer of Jesus helps us to meditate on this and to ask, 'Am I ready for heaven?' We need to ask ourselves this at all times, for we do not know the hour of our going.

As I write, a volcano in Congo has swallowed up the lives of hundreds. In 2001 in New York tragedy struck like lightning for 3,000 people. These are reminders that our lives are fragile, and we need to be ready. Some, at these times of terror, had time to say, 'Into your hands I commit my spirit.' Many others, in terminal illness or old age, will know that the time has come to put their house in order and prepare to die. In this brief but deep moment on the cross, Christ shows us the way. He shows us that we can make careful provision for our family, as he entrusts his mother to his friend John: 'Dear woman, here is your son . . . Here is your mother.' He shows that there can be reconciliation: 'Father, forgive them for they do not know what they are doing.' Jesus prays for his enemies' forgiveness, a theme we looked at in the Lord's Prayer in Chapter 5. As well as giving forgiveness as Jesus did, it may also be that we need to receive forgiveness from those who may have something against us. This is one of the things David Watson did before he died. His description is worth quoting in full.

> *On Advent Sunday morning I had a bad asthma attack. But during it, God spoke to me so powerfully and painfully that I have never felt so broken before him (and still do). He showed me that all my preaching, writing and other ministry was absolutely nothing compared to my love-relationship with him. In fact sheer busyness had squeezed out the close intimacy I had known during the first few months of the year after my operation.*
>
> *God also showed me that my 'love' for him meant nothing unless I was truly able to love from my heart my brother or sister in Christ. As the Lord put various names into my mind, I began to write letters to about twelve people asking for forgiveness for hurting them, for still being inwardly angry against them – or whatever. It was the most painful purging and pruning I can remember in my entire Christian life. But fruitful! Already some replies to my letters have reduced me to tears.*
>
> *Whatever else is happening to me physically, God is*

working deeply in my life . . . I am not now clinging on to physical life (though I still believe the Lord can heal . . .) but I am clinging on to the Lord. I am ready to go and be with Christ which would be literally heaven. But I'm equally ready to stay, if that is what God wants.

'Father, not my will but yours.' In that position of security I have experienced his perfect love, a love that casts out fear.[14]

Having provided for his family and sought forgiveness for his enemies, Jesus now entrusts his spirit into the hands of God: 'Father, into your hands I commit my spirit' (Lk 23:46). When writing this chapter I had lunch with Kurt Maeder, who leads a vibrant church in Strasbourg. His wife went through a battle with cancer, and two years ago, Kurt suffered a heart attack and had triple bypass surgery out of the blue at the end of one summer holiday. He spoke of the dark terror that the threat of death brought to him so unexpectedly in his hospital bed. Talking to him, and to others who have passed near to death, perhaps through a disease or accident, I have often heard them speak of this shadow that brings them out in a cold sweat. People testify to suddenly being dominated by fear and insecurity. The psalmist describes it: 'The cords of death encompassed me, the torrents of destruction overwhelmed me. The cords of the grave coiled around me; the snares of death confronted me' (Ps 18:4–5). He speaks also of 'the gates of death', 'the sleep of death', 'the dust of death', 'the valley of the shadow of death'. He expresses in graphic images what many go through: 'My heart is in anguish within me; the terrors of

[14] David Watson, *Fear No Evil* (Hodder & Stoughton, 1984) p. 171. David was one of the giants of the church in England in my generation. He died of cancer in his fifties, torn away from us so prematurely.

death assail me' (Ps 55:4). Or again: 'The cords of death entangled me, the anguish of the grave came upon me; I was overcome by trouble and sorrow' (Ps 116:3). In the light of this, we can be encouraged that such fear is common. We are, after all, face to face with the last enemy, death. But what are we to do?

Commenting on this theme, John White remarks on what a difference it makes knowing what you have to do in an emergency. He tells the story of when the air raid sirens first sounded when he was a boy. He was not afraid, because he knew exactly what to do: get dressed, wake the family and join them in the air raid shelter, where there were then other tasks to perform. If we find ourselves locked in a dungeon of doubt and fear, with the warning of death ringing in our ears, what can we do?

A phrase I love from *The Pilgrim's Progress* is this: 'I have a key in my bosom called *promise* which will, I am persuaded, open any lock in Doubting Castle.'[15] And it is at times like these that we need to understand the power of the promises of Christ. They truly are keys to set us free, if we can use them. In this case, the promise we can turn to is this: 'I tell you the truth, whoever hears my word and believes him who sent me has eternal life and will not be condemned; he has crossed over from death to life' (Jn 5:24).

With the phrase 'Into your hands I commit my spirit' it is as if Jesus holds the key towards us. This is an act of faith, an act of surrender, an act of trust which we can perform as part of the discipline of intimacy. It will be a disciplined act. It involves taking hold of the promises of eternal life, fulfilling their conditions and believing them. It involves believing Christ and joining ourselves to him. As we do so we will be given grace even to pass through the valley of the shadow of death without losing our dependence on the Father.

---

[15] John Bunyan, *The Pilgrim's Progress* (Edtn Strachan, 1858) p. 129.

In the same way that the Lord's Prayer can be used as a pattern for prayer, so we can follow these seven steps. Having come into the presence of God through worship, repentance and forgiveness, having climbed into a place of being 'seated with Christ', we can intercede with these seven burdens of Christ:

1. For the protection of the saints;
2. For the holiness of the saints;
3. For the love and unity of the saints;
4. For the witness and mission of the saints;
5. That we may see his glory;
6. That we may abandon ourselves to the Father's will;
7. That we may abandon our spirit into the Father's hands.

We can follow and pray these themes to stretch out our hands to God daily on behalf of our families, our children, our church, our leaders, our nation, and the nations.

HABAKKUK'S STORY

How long, O Lord, must I call for help, but you do not listen? Or cry out to you, 'Violence!' but you do not save? Why do you make me look at injustice? Why do you tolerate wrong? Destruction and violence are before me; there is strife, and conflict abounds. Therefore the law is paralysed, and justice never prevails. The wicked hem in the righteous, so that justice is perverted.

I will stand at my watch and station myself on the ramparts; I will look to see what he will say to me, and what answer I am to give to this complaint. Then the Lord replied:

'Write down the revelation and make it plain on tablets so that a herald may run with it. For the revelation awaits an appointed time; it speaks of the end and will not prove false. Though it linger, wait for it; it will certainly come and will not delay.'

A prayer of Habakkuk the prophet . . . Lord, I have heard of your fame; I stand in awe of your deeds, O Lord. Renew them in our day, in our time make them known; in wrath remember mercy.

Though the fig-tree does not bud and there are no grapes on the vines, though the olive crop fails and the fields produce no food, though there are no sheep in the pen and no cattle in the stalls, yet I will rejoice in the Lord, I will by joyful in God my Saviour.

The Sovereign Lord is my strength; he makes my feet like the feet of a deer, he enables me to go on the heights.
(Hab 1:2–4; 2:1–4, 20; 3:1–7, 17–19)

13

When God Is Silent

'Into the darkness of the night
With heartache kindled into love,
O blessed chance!
I went out unobserved,
My house being wrapped in sleep . . .

O night that led me, guiding night,
O night far sweeter than the dawn;
O night that did so then unite
The lover with his Beloved,
Transforming lover in Beloved.'

(St John of the Cross)[1]

'And in the midst of their merriment and tears the clear voice of a singer rose like silver and gold, and all men were hushed. And he sang to them . . . until their hearts, wounded with sweet words, overflowed, and their joy was like swords, and they passed in thought out to regions where pain and delight flow together and tears are the very wine of blessedness.'

(J. R. R. Tolkien)[2]

---

[1] St John of the Cross, *The Dark Night of the Soul* (Hodder & Stoughton, 1988), p. 1.

[2] J. R. R. Tolkien, *The Return of the King* (George Allen and Unwin, 1955), p. 232. There are many echoes of the Christian faith that Tolkien had in *The Lord of the Rings*, although most are hidden.

There are times in our lives when we are confronted by chaos and everything seems out of joint. We are struck by tragedy, threatened by disease or disaster, our deep longings are frustrated. Time is passing and we are not seeing the answers to our prayers. God is silent or is saying no, and we can't understand it. These experiences may go on for years and years. What are we to do? How should we cling on to the discipline of intimacy in these times of winter for our souls?

This is a question that no book on prayer should fail to address, yet the answer is not simple – at least, no simpler than the answer that was eventually given to Job. The comforters offered him reasons why tragedy had happened and why God was not answering. They reckoned it was to do with his sin. But he resisted, knowing that it was not there that the answer lay. In the end, the Lord answered Job out of the storm and it was through this encounter with God that an answer came which ultimately satisfied. Yet it took time.

The book of James gives one answer as to why many prayers remain unanswered, or why the answer is no. James says, 'You do not have, because you do not ask God. When you ask, you do not receive, because you ask with wrong motives, that you may spend what you get on your pleasures' (Jas 4:2–3). It is true that many times we need to return to God and examine our motives for asking. James adds, 'Don't you know that friendship with the world is hatred towards God?' We need to become friendly with God and to discover his desires for our lives and let them become our own desires. The psalmist's promise – 'Delight yourself in the Lord and he will give you the desires of your heart' (Ps 37:4) – becomes true as our desires are conformed to God's. Perhaps this happened for Hannah in those long years of praying for a child. In the end she came to the place where she could say, 'I will lend him to the Lord,' and so her prayer was answered.

According to James, we do not have because we do not

ask. It is true that often we have not sought God consistently in the way James had in mind. Later he says that the prayer of a righteous man is fervent and effective, going on to cite Elijah and his prayer for drought and then for rain (Jas 5:16–18 RSV). I remember being with John Mulinde at a 'prophetic breakfast' we used to hold in our church. It was asked why God was apparently answering prayer in Uganda and transforming the nation, whereas in France the church was struggling. John thought for a moment and then began to talk to us about fervency as the Africans understand it. He told us of deep times of consecration of his life 'on the altar' where he had done business with God about his own motivations and where his own security lay. Unquestionably, these times had borne fruit.

You may have had different times in your life where you have walked through the desert or the valley of the shadow of death. In our church we had those who were fighting with cancer, which at times receded then suddenly increased, like an inevitable sentence of death. The prayers of the saints were redoubled, but they were shaken. In our city we had friends struggling against a creeping, debilitating muscular disease. We often sensed the presence of the Holy Spirit as we prayed with them, but things did not get better. Healing has not come yet, and as the hope of having children recedes, they are tempted to ask, Where is God? Or: How long, O Lord?

I can think of times of barrenness in my own life. I recently re-read the journal I kept for the year following the death of my son Samuel at only nine weeks old in 1982. Often, for days at a time, there was a struggle to survive and to 'hold on to God' who seemed so far off. Here is an extract:

31 Jan: To church this morning in a drab agony. Unable to worship, I rather blame God. Sit through till lunch wondering if this might be the end of my call, my faith. Bitter against God for taking Samuel. I think when people talk about seeing miracles, how come no one trusted in God to raise Samuel from the dead? I am bitter about the credibility gap between the words, words, words of preachers, and the prayers . . . and the fact that nothing happens. I feel sick at heart at all this and give no comfort to Annie who bears all bravely.

13 Feb: Rainy day. Three whole long empty Samuel-less weeks. Ah, is it possible that this missing him, this longing for him can be getting stronger? I have not forgotten my angel boy for one moment of this long, long, aching day.

31 Mar: Poor dear Annie is so sad these days. It is as if we go back to square one sometimes and mourn for little Samuel as if it were only a day or two ago that he left us. God, my Lord, please be a holy Comforter to her.

Some reading these lines are no doubt also fighting for their faith in situations where the 'silence of God' is a daily challenge, and where there seems no answer. In these valleys, which sometimes last for so long, what are we to do?

The thesis of this book is, as the title suggests, that our hope lies in maintaining intimacy with God. Indeed, in these times we should even increase it. As we shall see from Habakkuk, we are called to station ourselves before the Lord in these times, and to seek his face. The comfort of others is a great solace, and sometimes people can bring a true word from God which brings us strength. We need to continue meeting together and keeping fellowship. But sometimes the well-meaning comfort of the saints is about as useful as that of Job's comforters. In those times, we need to break through to intimacy with God. We may indeed find that the only comfort is in God, but he is a true and real source of comfort. Let's move in close to the prophet Habakkuk to understand this all-important theme with which we close this book.

Habakkuk, a contemporary of Jeremiah, wrestled with God about the coming judgement on his nation, but he saw no answer. 'This account of wrestling with God, however, is not just a fragment from a private journal that has somehow entered the public domain. It was composed for Israel . . . struggling to comprehend the ways of God. God's answers therefore spoke to all who shared Habakkuk's troubled doubts.'[3]

Questioning

How long, O Lord, must I call for help, but you do not listen? Or cry out to you, 'Violence!' but you do not save? Why do you make me look at injustice? Why do you tolerate wrong? Destruction and violence are before me; there is strife, and conflict abounds. Therefore the law is paralysed, and justice never prevails. The wicked hem in the righteous, so that justice is perverted. (Hab 1:2–4)

Habakkuk's complaint is common to many who are intimate with God. Indeed, we could almost say that it is an essential component of the life of someone who prays with vigour. For God seeks those who will be real with him, and he takes them down paths where they are obliged to walk by faith and not by sight. We think of the complaint of Abraham waiting for a son; of Moses in the desert without food or water; of Hannah; of David saying, 'Out of the depths, O Lord, I cry to you.' They were all asking, 'Why? How long?' Apparently these are legitimate questions to ask in prayer!

---

[3] *NIV Study Bible* (Hodder & Stoughton, 1985) p. 1362.

Seeing

Habakkuk is then given a vision that he does not appreciate, difficult as it is to understand. It seems that God will answer by making things worse, and by executing judgement through the ruthless Babylonians. But the destroyer will be destroyed – in the end. Habakkuk learns to rest in God's plans in a spirit of waiting in hope and in worship.

> *I will stand at my watch and station myself on the ramparts; I will look to see what he will say to me, and what answer I am to give to this complaint. Then the Lord replied: 'Write down the revelation and make it plain on tablets so that a herald may run with it. For the revelation awaits an appointed time; it speaks of the end and will not prove false. Though it linger, wait for it; it will certainly come and will not delay.' (Hab 2:1–3)*

In times of perplexity, let us seek the face of God. Surely these times are given for us to hold on to him, and as we do, even if we are perplexed we will grow in the knowledge of him. These times can then be times of gaining a vision of God and of his plans. And if it linger and we have to wait, the time will not be wasted.

Remembering, standing, trembling

> *Lord, I have heard of your fame; I stand in awe of your deeds, O Lord. Renew them in our day, in our time make them known; in wrath remember mercy. (Hab 3:2)*

These themes of remembering, standing in the presence of God, which we have seen before are beautifully expressed in these prayers. 'Lord, I have heard of your fame.' As we pray in times of distress, we do well to rehearse the mighty deeds of God – in his word, in times of revival and in our lives. Just as John said, 'Remember the height from which you have fallen,' so Habakkuk is remembering the fame of the Lord. He then 'stands in awe'. I picture him, with his eyes lifted heavenwards, proclaiming the character and the deeds of God. We will find as we do this, even when there is no specific answer to our request, that we are edified and built up and we grow in the knowledge of God. Like Moses, Joel, Isaiah, Jesus and Paul, Habakkuk too has a vision of the radiance of God. Those intimate with God can expect this; Jesus prayed for it, the disciples spoke of it, the prophets were silenced by it. And it often happens during the times when God appears silent.

Here is Habakkuk's vision of the glory: 'God came from Teman, the Holy One from Mount Paran. His glory covered the heavens and his praise filled the earth. His splendour was like the sunrise; rays flashed from his hand, where his power was hidden.'

The revelation comes with an awareness of doom. Like Job, who at the sound of the Lord repents in dust and ashes; like Isaiah and John the Divine, who fall on their faces like those dead, Habakkuk the intercessor trembles and stops his striving, resigning himself to waiting. 'He stood and shook the earth; he looked, and made the nations tremble . . . I heard and my heart pounded, my lips quivered at the sound; decay crept into my bones, and my legs trembled. Yet I will wait patiently for the day of calamity to come on the nation invading us' (Hab 2:6, 16).

Waiting

Habakkuk says, 'I will wait patiently.' He says: 'I will stand at my watch and station myself on the ramparts.' For those who have no answer to their prayer, this is a high calling.

Psalm 130:5 says: 'I wait for the Lord, my soul waits, and

in his word I put my hope.' In a moment of insight Isaiah says, 'I will wait for the Lord, who is hiding his face from the house of Jacob. I will put my trust in him' (Is 8:17). He later gives great encouragement to those in need of perspective: 'Those who hope in the Lord shall renew their strength. They will soar on wings like eagles; they will run and not grow weary, they will walk and not faint' (Is 40:31). Lamentations adds: 'The Lord is good to those whose hope is in him, to the one who seeks him. It is good to wait quietly for the salvation of the Lord' (Lam 3:25–26).

The vital message is: those who are in a time of apparent impasse should not give up, but should with renewed vigour wait for the Lord. Paul says that we 'groan inwardly as we wait eagerly for our adoption as sons, the redemption of our bodies . . . But if we hope for what we do not yet have, we wait for it patiently' (Rom 8:23, 25). This is such an encouragement for those who are physically unwell, but it also speaks to those seeking revival in a nation. Around the time of the coming of Jesus, we get the impression of a cluster of people waiting, watching, longing, praying. One such, of course, was Simeon, 'who was righteous and devout. He was waiting for the consolation of Israel, and the Holy Spirit was upon him' (Lk 2:25). In these times, we wait for the Holy Spirit to come upon us and console us.

Worshipping

We come finally to verses of encouragement for those in periods of complete barrenness. And in a sense this book has come full circle. We end, as we began, with the call to intimacy, with the call to 'come back to our first love'. Habakkuk says: 'Though the fig-tree does not bud and there are no grapes on the vines, though the olive crop fails and the fields produce no food, though there are no sheep in the pen and no cattle in the stalls, yet I will rejoice in the Lord, I will be joyful in God my Saviour. The Sovereign Lord is my strength; he makes my feet like the feet of a deer, he enables me to go on the heights' (Hab 3:17–19).

Those who are looking for 'the consolation of Israel' can do just that. In the barren times, in the times of defeat, let us worship him! In times when there is no answer, where we have unresolved prayer, let us 'rejoice in the Lord'. In the times of bereavement, when things have not turned out as we expected, let us climb up to him! In times of doubt and sorrow and fear of the future, times of disappointment, let us, with Habakkuk, 'be joyful in God my Saviour'. As we do so, we may suddenly find ourselves, like the deer, on the heights. We may find ourselves in the place of true perspective, seated with him in heavenly places. We may find that God answers our prayer – or we may not. But let us fulfil the purpose for which we were created, namely to 'be for the praise of his glory'.

So we may find in this obedience of worship an answer to our prayer. This happened for Hannah. It happened also to my dear friend Guy Chevreau's wife. Guy is a preacher who travels extensively, teaching about the kingdom of God, but at some cost, as his wife has been so unwell. Janis supports Guy's ministry one hundred per cent, but her illness has been like a long nightmare. While writing this chapter I received her wonderful news which I reproduce here.

Twenty-three years ago I was diagnosed with what today has sadly become a common disease – fibromyalgia. At the time, however, not much was known about it. With each new specialist I saw, the words fell into a pattern: 'You are the worst case that I have seen'; 'Medically, there is nothing we can do to help you.'

These last two years have been a struggle simply to survive. The disease had left me in extreme exhaustion, with poor vision and balance, cognitive difficulties, and a severely depleted immune and central nervous system. Surgery and a minor accident last spring left me almost totally house-bound. Often I dressed at 3pm, so the children would see me up when they arrived home from school. This past November I spent most of the month unable to walk. The pain in my legs was excruciating, and to bear any weight on them felt as if my bones were being crushed. We feared that a wheel-chair was the next step, bringing with it yet another level of adjustment.

God in his great mercy has carried me minute by minute through years of pain, loss, grief and isolation, and I know there is wisdom that can be learned only in the crucible. Still, most of the time, life seemed too hard to endure, and with sadness I often found myself asking God to take me home, so that I could run and dance with Jesus, free of pain at last, and my family could be free to taste life more fully.

We've prayed, fasted, and begged to awaken from this nightmare. We have been privileged to receive wonderful ministry over the years – inner healing, physical healing, deliverance, prophetic discernment – and we tried to turn every key we felt God initiate. So many, all over the world, have prayed for me for so many years and, with humility and great gratitude, we know that these prayers have sustained us.

When the Spirit dwells in us, he bestows righteousness, peace and joy. My faith in the sovereignty of God was strong. I loved Jesus and knew that he loved me. I had been as faithful and obedient as I had received grace for. Peace wasn't the problem either. There were no questions – they had been exhausted years ago. I had simply adopted a statement of faith that 'Since nothing could touch me that didn't have to first pass through the hand of God, this must then be of God.' What I continuously struggled to find was joy. 'Hope deferred . . .' had become my signature verse. I had ridden the rollercoaster of hope and disappointment for years and it had left me heart-sick.

In November I tuned in to the TACF[4] *Healing Conference over the Internet, as physically I was unable to get there any more. My head said not to, to protect myself, but my heart was being nudged. With the first session there came an instant paradigm shift. God clearly let me know that I had been believing many subtle religious lies about my healing, which had taken root over years of wear and tear. Over the next few days, the Holy Spirit kept bringing to my attention careless words and judgements spoken, and skewed misunderstandings of the nature of God that I had adopted concerning healing. I spent a lot of time repenting and poring through the gospels, reading every account of healing. I clearly saw that God didn't need me stuck at home in tears and pain to be glorified! He could surely find far better ways to teach and use me!*

When my husband returned home from Mexico I insisted that he listen to the conference sessions. We were both very drawn to one of the speakers, Bill Johnson, and his teaching on the kingdom and healing. After a few phone calls, we arranged to fly across the continent to meet with him and a ministry team at the church. In the natural, it was ridiculous to make such a trip – at home, I could hardly climb a single flight of stairs. But there had grown in me such a serious hatred of the enemy for all of his robbery, and the Lord had simultaneously deposited great passion and boldness to fight to see his kingdom come. There were so many pieces of the puzzle that amazingly fell into place that we felt supernaturally encouraged. To be awakened to hope in God again was beyond wonderful! A light was shining in my darkness – it could only be God!

The church in Redding welcomed and honoured us, and we experienced Christ through them. At mid-point in the weekend, one of the pastors received a dream wherein he saw

---

[4] Toronto Airport Christian Fellowship.

a large dragon wrapped around my body. He understood it as a generational witchcraft curse, designed to come against ministry.

Quite quickly and easily those praying for me untangled this 'thing' from my upper body and I felt an instant relief of pain in my back and neck. Yet with this relief came an intense pain in one leg. When I mentioned this I was told that the creature had a very long claw latched through my thigh in an effort to hold fast to its loosening grip. When the team grabbed on and pulled the claw out, I felt a ripping through my leg and was instantly pain free.

One of the team then asked me if I would like to try walking around, so we set off around the sanctuary, hand in hand. Not far along she asked me if I would like to try running. The words 'Oh no, I don't run!' came out of my mouth immediately, as a formed response. As quickly as they came, I heard the Lord's question: 'Why don't you run?' I repeated those four words out loud, and began to run and run and run. After three laps around an 800-seat room, I stopped for two reasons: I was out of breath, and I was in shock. I had just witnessed a miracle that could never be denied! My husband began to weep, for in almost 20 years of marriage, he had never seen me run.

Since that day, just over a month ago, I have been able to stand for hours at a time. I am going for 20-minute walks most days; and I am dancing with Jesus in worship every day, all of which were previously impossible. As I worship I am drawn into the presence of Jesus and I am strengthened in body and spirit each time I do so. As I walk, my spirit soars and I feel God's great pleasure. I often fling open my arms and do a spin on the streets! I am baby-stepping back into the wonders of life that God has created for our enjoyment.

God has restored my wellspring of joy! I am constantly overwhelmed by the supreme goodness of God, and his delight in me. Each day I awake and ask to see his goodness pass before my eyes – and every day I see it multiplied. I have been awakened in my spirit and am captivated by him!

In the book of Revelation, we are told that when we get to heaven, God will wipe away every tear. I have often wondered what that will look like. Could I ever forget my long years of suffering? Now I am honestly able to say that those tears have already been wiped clean and are as if they never were. Hope and joy have been renewed. This is by far my greatest miracle!

To those of you who are still waiting and watching for the Lord's physical touch on your body, take God at his word. 'Tears may last for a night – but joy comes in the morning.' I cannot tell you how long your night will be, but I do know that joy will *dawn as he has promised!*

It is difficult to convey the renewed hope that is within me, for it far transcends what has happened to me physically. I have not experienced an instant fountain of youth as I thought that healing might bring! My muscles are severely deconditioned, but I am being strengthened day by day. There are still lingering symptoms that restrict me – but I have tasted of his pleasure and kingdom power, and I know that God is absolutely faithful to complete that which he has begun in me. Joy is bubbling and I am head-over-heels in love!

All to his glory and honour.

Janis Chevreau

I remember times spent with Guy in Paris, and at his home in Toronto, where I listened with my heart pounding as I heard of the struggle and the fight that Janis was having to pass through, and which was inevitably affecting the whole family. I shook my head and asked, 'How long? Why?' And now it seems we have the answer – at least to the 'How long?'. But I want to commend the long period of waiting to your attention. The disease was diagnosed twenty-three years ago. Long years of uncertainty and recently several years of acute pain and incapacity. And during this time, Janis sought the Lord and kept intimate with him. She kept poised before him, as did Guy. Even though there was no fruit of healing in their family, yet they praised him. They kept their discipline of intimacy. And they were rewarded. I write to those whose prayer in their family is as yet unanswered. I write for those who long for their nation to be healed. I write for those with paralysis in the home or in the church or in the nation, and I say, with Habakkuk, 'Though the fig-tree does not bud and there are no grapes on the vines, though the olive crop fails and the fields produce no food, though there are no sheep in the pen and no cattle in the stalls, yet I will rejoice in the Lord, I will be joyful in God my Saviour. The Sovereign Lord is my strength; he makes my feet like the feet of a deer, he enables me to go on the heights.'

I quoted at the start of this chapter from my prayer journal of twenty years ago, the year that our son Samuel died. It was a time of trial and a time of unanswered prayer. After a while I began to understand this secret of praise. The following is a love letter to Christ I wrote during those months. I think it is a fitting way to end this book, as we endeavour to be waiting and worshipping in the presence of the Father:

> *8 June: A. W. Tozer said, 'It is rare to find anyone aglow with personal love for Christ. This love, as a kind of moral fragrance, is ever detected on the garments of the saints. The list of fragrant saints is long. It includes men and women of every theological shade of theological thought within the bounds of orthodox Christian faith. This radiant love for Christ is to my mind the test of true catholicity, the one sure proof of membership of the Church Universal.'*[5]

---

[5] A. W. Tozer, *The Pursuit of God* (Christian Publications, 1982).

I want to begin to put down here my love for you. I don't tell you nearly enough about it and I'm sorry. I remember how I first fell in love with you. I watched you walking in Galilee and in Jerusalem. I watched from afar but I had to come closer because all that you did was so beautiful. That's what I mean when I say that you are beautiful to me. All you did in spending your life for others . . . never being impatient, always being ready to help, to give food to the starving, to heal the crippled and the blind and to drive out demons and to set so many people's lives back on the course they had left so long, so long ago. I fell in love with your teaching, especially that God is a loving Father who has counted even the hairs on my head; that we need to lose our selfish life to find life in all its fullness; that the things of this world do not satisfy, but that you are the living water and if we drink, we'll never be thirsty. O, how I love you. I love your generosity, and your love; your provision for us in sending the Holy Spirit; your compassion, your understanding for man – you knew what was in man's heart. But I love your strength too, the way you hated our lying and pretending to love God more than we do. Jesus, I'm sorry for trying to appear to others something that I'm not. I dread being just another Pharisee.

Jesus I love you so much that I want to be with you, my Lord and my God. I want to spend my life in the service of others like you did. You did not stop when people turned against you. You pressed on in your love for men and women and for me so that in the end you were stripped of friends and clothes and everything; stripped, whipped and then pierced with hard nails; a bleeding, suffering servant of all. O, the breadth and height and length and depth of your love, my Lord and my God.

And in all this you were fighting with a different, older enemy, whom you were strong enough to trample under foot when you defeated death on the day of the resurrection.

> *9 June: I am hungering and thirsting after you. Like the deer longing for water. 'Sir, we would see Jesus.' How I would see you, my Lord and my God. It seems in so many lives that all we have is faint echoes from a distant thunder, so that men report news of something afar off. I feel so much like that. But I want to be close to you, to reach out and hug you, to give you a bear hug. The cry of my heart is to be close to you. For this I know I must let go any sin and seek you. Please, O please, Lord Jesus, be found by me! Or let me be found by you. For away from you I'm like a life raft cut loose from its mother ship and tossed to pieces.*

My prayer is still the same, and I hope it is yours. Through the discipline of intimacy we want to know him and to love him and, by God's grace, to make him known. May God help you as you get to know him better.

APPENDIX 1

Visit to Prayer Mountain, Uganda

Stuart McAlpine, pastor of Christ Our Shepherd Church in Washington DC, mails a weekly pastoral letter to his flock. This is what he wrote on his return from a visit to John Mulinde's church in Kampala.

29 January 2002
Dearest family,
I arrived in Kampala about midnight Sunday evening, and the next morning, found my way on to the main drag through the city in search of the Trumpet Centre. Fine red dust; crippled beggars; swarms of 'boda bodas' (motorbikes); minibuses jammed to the roof; a myriad of stalls that carry every piece of non-utilitarian western plastic ware that you can imagine; soldiers and guns; the continuous blare of car horns; the smell of refuse in blocked open drains.

At the bottom of the hill, amidst a maze of shop-filled lanes, up a rough and rocky alley, I find what I am looking for. I negotiate a Toyota flatbed reversing towards me, crammed with armed militia. Stepping between piles of fruit skins, and the remains of last night's fires, I enter the sanctum.

Descending some high, cracked concrete steps, you find the sanctuary below ground level, like a military bunker for its own spiritual war. It has the feel of a crude barn to it – an apt comparison upon reflection – a veritable storehouse where harvest is gathered. As I think of the multi-million dollar western church complexes, complete with gym and theatre, I cannot help but think of Jeremiah's words, 'What has straw to do with grain?' This place is definitely granular.

There are 3 sections, 14 rows a section, and each section bench must seat about 6 people. It is the place you saw in the *Transformations* video, where the mist came down as the people travailed for their land. The interior is stark and bare, and all that hangs on the walls, breaking the uninterrupted expanse of cracked and stained cream paint, are homemade frames that announce in hand-written letters the nations of the earth. Above my head, in red letters, no fewer than 30 different Caribbean enclaves are cited. I have no doubt that each of them is well-known by even the illiterate here, simply because they are prayed for. Yet many a westerner would be hard pushed to compete with such geographical knowledge. It is the difference between knowing after the spirit and knowing after the flesh.

I cannot resist the desire to move and sit myself beneath the frame announcing USA and CANADA. I reach towards it to symbolically receive something of the overflow of the flood of prayer that has arisen from here for our nation. Around me there are others who have come to pray, and over the next three hours, a stream of men and women come and go. To my left, a thin man in his thirties travails, changing position from his bench to kneeling at the platform without a break in his incessant pleading. Raised hands and rocking bodies keep the rhythm for the murmurings and crying.

Here is a maturity of spirit amidst primitive space; here is a fertility of heart amidst a barrenness of physical supply. This is the Trumpet Centre, so named after Joel 2:1: 'Blow the trumpet . . .' the text which is emblazoned above the platform, calling people to be both ready and right for the coming of the Lord. This building is immediately behind the Crane Bank, one of the more prestigious banks in Kampala, and one of the most dominating structures. And yet this humble sanctuary, in the shadow of these evidences of the principalities and powers, calls into question their control, as the hymn of God's sovereignty and the declaration of his reign are pronounced without ceasing.

The rest of my time was spent on Prayer Mountain. The thrill of being at prayer for the nations with 1,500 Ugandans for an eight-hour prayer meeting will remain a highlight. How they pray for us in the USA and the UK. The hill is covered with little orange pup-tents for those who stay there day and night to intercede. Little groups of pray-ers can be seen dotted across the hillside, gently swaying as they implore heaven for others. There were about 300 internationals there. I didn't in fact meet another American, though I'm sure there had to be others. The Europeans were mainly German, Austrian and British, all of whose lands had been mightily impacted by the fruit of Uganda's ministry. We prayed through the nations, particularly these ones. A large flag of the nation would be brought to the platform and the congregation would rise to respond to the Ugandan pastor leading the intercession.

We are equally called to be a house of prayer for the nations. I have returned with a burden for Uganda that makes me weep to think about it. I walked away from the meeting place one day and looked back at them all. I read the newspapers every day I was there and realised how close to the surface of political life are the old demons that butchered this nation. There's hardly anyone whose family did not know the machete of Amin's terror. And as I looked at them all, faces shining with joy and sanctity, I wondered about their future, and prayed for their preservation. The history of martyrdom is a deep one in this place.

There is so much loose talk about 'the anointing'. In this

nation, the anointing for many was an 'anointing unto burial'. Do we want the anointing? At one point in a session, the microphones went dead. The PA system was down. I found myself smiling to myself in a wistful way. PA summed it up here – P for PURITY and A for AUTHORITY. This was their PA system – this was the power of their communication. This was the amplification for their message and convictions.

Before I left, I deliberately did not ask anyone to speak as I believed that following the previous Sunday it was important to gather for corporate prayer. Sunday morning is the best time to get everyone at the same place for the same purpose. May we respond with ever increasing fervency and faithful obedience to the call of God to simply ASK. How desperate it is to not have because we never asked. I encourage you to be unashamed and unstinting in your pursuit of God. His ear is not deaf that it cannot hear. Even so come to our nation, O Lord!

Pastorally yours,

Stuart McAlpine

APPENDIX 2

Prophecies for Different Nations

Prophecy given by Jean Darnall in the 1970s – Revival touching Britain and Europe

'I saw the British Isles glistening like a clump of jade in the grey seas surrounding them. It was a bird's-eye view. Looking down I saw Scotland, England, Wales and to the north west, Ireland. The tree tops upon the hills and the clustered clouds hid the people. Suddenly, small flickering lights appeared. They were scattered all over the isles. I came closer to the land. The light was fire-light. There were fires burning from the top of Scotland to Land's End, the tip of Cornwall. Lightning streaked downward from the sky above me. I saw it touch down with lightning swiftness, exploding each of the fires into streams of light. Like lava, they burned their fiery path downward from the top of Scotland to Land's End. The waters did not stop them, but the fire spread across the seas to Ireland and to Europe.

'The streams of fiery light into Europe seemed to be an army of all types of people, moving into the continent with a compassionate ministry. This ministry was not mass meetings, led by powerful personalities, preaching to spectators; but participating, caring communities involved with each other at grass roots level, sharing the love of God everywhere. I saw the empty cradles of Europe, her churches, holding a new generation of Christian leaders.

'I began to perceive God had more to say about the rivers of fire that would flow across the English Channel and over Europe. The word "communicators" kept coming to mind as I prayed. Communicators? That was a new word for ministry. God calls missionaries, evangelists. Does he call communicators? . . .

'I could see the dark cathedrals of Europe light up.'

Prophecy given by John Mulinde for Britain

'I saw the map of the continent of Europe and as I looked, there came out of this map a big pillar of smoke. It was a tall, thick and dark pillar of heavy black fumes as from a factory chimney. The fumes rose up very slowly and gradually began spreading out.

'From the pillar came a thin mist and it began spreading out almost imperceptibly, but within a short time it had formed a dark film over the entire continent of Europe. As the mist grew thicker, the features below it blurred and became difficult to distinguish under the film of black fumes.

'Then, suddenly, I saw a small light spring out from within the isles of the UK. It grew rapidly with finger-like rays of light spreading out in all directions. The rays of the south spread out wider and with longer beams than the rest and cut across the European mainland. For some time they disappeared into the thick black cloud rising and spreading over the rest of Europe; then they broke through and reappeared from within the fumes. They spread out even further, touching across the entire African continent, eastwards across North and South America. Then the picture disappeared and in its place came a scripture:

Arise, shine, for your light has come, and the glory of the Lord rises upon you. See, darkness covers the earth and thick darkness is over the peoples, but the Lord rises upon you and his glory appears over you. Nations will come to your light, and kings to the brightness of your dawn. [Is 60:1–3, NIV]

Lift up thine eyes round about, and see: they all gather themselves together, they come to thee: thy sons shall come from far, and thy daughters be nursed at thy side.

Then thou shalt see, and flow together, and thine heart shall fear, and be enlarged; because the abundance of the sea shall be converted unto thee, the forces of the Gentiles shall come unto thee. [Is 60:4–5, AV]

'A thick darkness is rising over the continent of Europe. It is going to grow in intensity and will soon cover the whole continent and on to the rest of the world. It is a force of evil. Wherever it will gain full control over any land, it will turn the hearts of the people totally away from God. They will hate anything to do with God, with righteousness or indeed with any goodness. Sanity will be cast overboard, and people will call good evil and evil good. They will desire to give vent to the basest animal passions in them and will look for wilder and wilder ways of doing this. They will enjoy evil and will love all others who enjoy it.

'The light is my power of renewal soon to be released upon the land and people of Europe. It will come if my people give themselves wholeheartedly to seeking my face. Its coming will be like a great storm. It will be a mighty power against the darkness and will protect my people from the effect of the invasion of darkness. Wherever the light will break out the darkness shall be neutralised and defeated. But this calls for the co-operation of my people in seeking for it to happen.

Arise, shine, for your light has come, and the glory of the Lord rises upon you. See, darkness covers the earth and thick darkness is over the peoples, but the Lord rises upon you and his glory appears over you. Nations will come to your light, and kings to the brightness of your dawn'. (Isaiah 60:1–3)

'The Lord is calling Britain into a special place of responsibility. A great light will spring out of the UK. It will . . . sweep across the whole of Europe like a bush fire. Indeed, it will stretch out to the ends of the world where it will join with other fires in worldwide revival.

'If you will answer this call, O Britain, and give yourself to institute prayer in your land . . . And seek the Lord with all your heart . . . With groaning and travailing prayer, even as a woman in labour pains; yes, if you will repent of your sins and iniquities, if you will heal the wounded hearts within you and cause unity to abound among your people; oh, if you will return to your redemptive purpose and again be faithful to the work of being a witness of the gospel in the nations. Then God will release upon you a mighty outpouring of his Spirit. You will again be clothed with the glory of the Lord. You will be a nation that bears the name of the Lord like a banner in the sky.

'Other nations will see what God is doing in you. Yes, those who are struggling against the domineering darkness looming over their territories will call light and redemption to many, even as in the olden days. That is God's redemptive purpose for you.

'If you will rise up to the challenge then the Lord will use you to take light to such as these. Then, even if the rising darkness covers their land, they will survive its destructive influence because of the revival power of God. Such is the responsibility that God is laying upon you: to bring the revival that will spread out to the rest of Europe.

'If you do not rise up to your calling, God will cause judgement to fall upon you, Britain, for having neglected and forsaken your destiny as a great missionary nation, and for not paying heed to what God offered you as an opportunity of grace (Proverbs 1:22–33).

'For it was God's plan from the beginning to use you to take the Good News to the nations of the world. That is why from the beginning he allowed you great authority as a maritime nation: that you may travel far and wide.

'It was his hand that allowed you to establish an empire covering almost the entire world. It was not just for your pride but so that, in the process, you may win over the peoples of those nations to him. Yes, it was even him that blessed your language – English – into becoming the most widely spoken language in the world. He intended to use it as a medium of communication, effectively linking the peoples of the world.

'"Look, your sons and daughters come from afar and gather themselves to you" (Isaiah 60:4–5). From the Americas, Africa, Asia and Australia. They will again form a holy alliance with you and in this networking great and mighty things shall come to pass.

'Many will come from Africa and the rest of the "third world" and will be used by the Lord to bless you spiritually. In some places they will take over your abandoned places of worship and will bring new life into them and great blessing in revival. That is why the Lord says in Isaiah 60:5: "Then you shall see, and flow together, and your heart shall fear, and be enlarged."

'This will demand great humbling on your part, but God shall lift you up. These are the last days and God is calling every nation to take its position in God's redemptive purposes and fulfil God's calling. Nor are you the last. Do not let pride hinder you. Look at the gifting God has allowed you to acquire over the years, and the unique position you hold in relation to Europe, America, Africa and indeed Asia. Turn now and do not allow yourself to miss God's timing.

All Europe is going to pass through a very painful struggle between two aggressive forces – light versus darkness! God has called you to play a crucial role. SO ARISE!'

Prophetic word given by Rick Joyner: the French anointing

'I believe a few years ago the Lord showed me that the next great watershed move of God was going to come through the French-speaking people. The Lord has uniquely called different nations for different purposes, and has given them different gifts. Each one reflects his glory in a different way. Every one of the apostles that the Lord called was very different from the others. Every prophet in the Scriptures was unique. They each had a different piece of the puzzle.

'I stumbled upon a phrase one time in a church history book, then I kept seeing it over and over in other history books, that referred to the apostles Peter, Paul and John as the three pillars of the church. All of these three were very different from one another, but they all had a very significant part in laying the foundation of the church. I believe that all the apostles had a part, along with all the prophets, in laying the foundations of the church. But these three are repeatedly referred to as pillars of the church. They certainly seem to have the most significant part in laying the foundation of the church.

'Then I started thinking about these three in relation to church history. If we look at the nature of Peter, he was very impetuous and unstable. He was prone to breathtaking victories and heart-rending mistakes. If you look at church history, we see Peter probably having the greatest influence in the very beginning. For over 1,000 years the emphasis was on Peter and his ministry. Those in leadership in the church claimed to be seated on the seat of Peter. The church of that period seemed very much to have the nature of Peter. Extraordinary victories and advances for the gospel were followed by some extraordinary mistakes. But the Lord used that church as much as he could.

'Then we have the beginning of the Reformation. The Reformation began with a rediscovery of the epistles of Paul; a rediscovery of the epistle to the Romans. Since then, for over 500 years, most of the emphasis of the church has been the epistles of Paul. We have definitely needed that emphasis again in the church.

'But John had the last word. I believe that we are going to come to a final phase of church history where we see the emphasis of John becoming the main emphasis of the church. It doesn't mean that we forget Peter and Paul. But I believe we are going to see ascending again to the forefront John's message, that we should love the Lord and love one another.

'In a sense you could see the three of them representing the Way, the Truth and the Life. We need to understand the Way. We need an absolute devotion to Truth. But if we don't know Jesus as our Life, we don't really know the Way or the Truth either. We need all three together, but I believe that a great emphasis is coming upon the last of these: seeing Jesus as our Life.

'It seems very fitting that when the Lord called John, he was mending nets. Just as we see the gospel of John tying the other gospels together, and the epistles of John tying the New Testament together, the book of Revelation that he wrote ties the entire Scriptures together and finishes them off. I believe that his ministry and his message are just going to tie everything together, so that the harvest, which is the end of the age, can finally be gathered.

'John was the one who leaned his head on the Lord's breast. He could hear the heartbeat of God as he leant on his breast. It is one thing to have the mind of Christ, but we must also have his heart. It's not a matter of just doing the right things. If we have his heart, we will do them for the right reasons. He requires truth in the innermost being. It is not just by believing in our minds that we find righteousness, but also by believing in our heart.

'When I first went to France, I tried to study France as much as I could. It looked to me like there had been a resistance to moves of God throughout the French history, or a resistance to new moves of God, resistance to things that were different or unique. And yet the Lord showed me that the French were going to lead in the last-day move of God. I started to understand right away how this could happen. When you go to France, it seems that the whole culture is based around relationship. They sit at meals for hours and hours. The wine flows. But everything is based around relationships. I could see that when some of the Reformation's truths are preached there, the French people would say, "So what?" because they don't see lives that reflect that truth.

'But I also began to understand how the message of John alone, based on relationships – loving the Lord and loving each other – could reach the French people . . . and reach the ends of the earth.'

Study Guide

Introduction

The questions listed below can be used for personal study and reflection or in a small group setting. If in a group, times of prayer are often suggested. It is probably wise to have these after your discussion of all the questions has concluded.

It is strongly recommended that you buy a page-a-day diary or prayer journal. Many questions involve listing things or writing prayers. It is a help to do this in your journal.

Chapter 1 – Coming Back to Our First Love

Texts: Revelation 2:1–7; Song of Songs 2:10–13.

1. How do you find your rest in God?
2. Are you aware of a growing hunger for prayer around you? Give some examples.
3. Discuss any prayer event you've been to where you've experienced a 'spirit of prayer'.
4. What would it mean for your church to become a 'house of prayer for all nations'?
5. Do you have any experience of fasting? Do you want to?

6. Do you know of any example of a nation being changed by prayer?
7. Read the story of the Cleansing of the Temple (Luke 19:45–48). Do you feel that some things need to be driven from your life for it to become a 'house of prayer'? What things?

Chapter 2 – 'Remember the Height From Which You Have Fallen'

Texts: Revelation 2:1–7; Deuteronomy 8.

1. To what extent do you think it is inevitable that Christians will 'forsake their first love'?
2. What do you think the Ephesians' 'first love' was? (You can also refer to Acts 19, and Ephesians 1 and 2.)
3. Spend some time remembering the first time you fell in love. If appropriate, share the story.
4. Spend some time remembering the first time you experienced love for Jesus. Can you say what happened?
5. Have you at times abandoned the love you had at first? If so, why did that happen?
6. Revelation 2:5 talks of the 'height from which you have fallen'. What do you think is that height for you?
7. Read Ephesians 1. Which of the aspects of salvation that Paul lists is the most precious to you?
8. What do you think it means to be 'raised up with him and made to sit with him in heavenly places'?
9. If it is an experience, have you ever had it?
10. Do you aspire to it? If so, how might you go about attaining it?

Chapter 3 – The Discipline of Repentance

Texts: Revelation 2:1–7; Jeremiah 8:22–23; 9:16–21.

1. Do you think there is a 'gift of tears'? What is it?
2. Do you cry ever in church or prayer? Why? Why not?
3. What, in your opinion, has repentance got to do with tears?
4. What is repentance?
5. Do you think there is such a thing as the 'gift' of repentance?
6. What things may we need to repent of in the church today?
7. What things particularly cause prayerlessness in the church, for which we may need to repent?
8. Have you ever experienced a time of repentance in your life? Could you tell the story?
9. Are there things over which God is causing you to repent at this time?
10. If appropriate, share these with the group or in pairs and pray for one another.

Chapter 4 – 'Do the Things You Did at First'

Texts: Revelation 2:1–5; Acts 19.

1. Take some time to choose your time for a daily appointment with God. Communicate this with another person for mutual accountability.
2. What helps you personally to experience the presence of God?
3. Do you agree that it is rare to meet people who are 'in love' with God? Name some that you have met. What is their secret?
4. Write a love song to God.
5. How can we 'hear the voice of God'? How can you develop this capacity?
6. What is your experience of Bible meditation? How can you increase your capacity for this?

7. Resolve to obtain a prayer journal. In it, write a letter to the Father which expresses your current heart longings.
8. Read Isaiah 50:4. What ministry do you feel God is calling you to at this time? In what way has he spoken to you of this?

Chapter 5 – The Master Plan of Prayer

Text: Matthew 6:5–15.

1. Have you tried praying the Lord's Prayer in the manner described? What is your feeling about this discipline of prayer? Does it help you?
2. What is/has been most helpful/unhelpful to you in deepening your understanding of God as your Father?
3. Discuss the extent to which heaven is real or important to you. Does the hope of heaven affect your daily life? Should it?
4. How many names of God can you remember? How do you think we can 'hallow' them?
5. Try to define what, for you, the coming of the kingdom means. List as many different domains as you can in which you think the kingdom might come on earth as in heaven.
6. Do you find it easy or difficult to pray for material needs? Why? Have you had answers to prayer in this area? Tell the story.
7. In the 1904 Welsh revival, preacher Evan Roberts used to say, 'Have you forgiven everyone, everyone, everyone?' Think about and discuss those you have found it hard to forgive. What has to happen for it to be possible? Pray for one another, if appropriate.
8. How do you feel we best fight against evil and temptation? Name several things which can help.

9. Why do you think Jesus ends his prayer as he does? What can we do to live more in the kingdom, power and glory of God?
10. Spend some time praying through the Lord's Prayer. If in a group, try this together and give at least 30 minutes to it.

Chapter 6 – What Is intercession?

Text: Genesis 18:1–28.

1. 'To pray is to change.' Have you had the experience of being changed by prayer? In what way, and how did it happen?
2. Have you, like Abraham, ever had the experience of a revelation from God of what is going to happen? Do you believe this can happen? How can we guard against deception in this area?
3. Have you ever had this kind of dialogue with God? Do you think it is reserved only for the giants of the faith, or is it for everyone?
4. Can you think of any other biblical examples of prayer averting judgement?
5. Abraham held on to God in prayer over the judgement of a city, and would not let go. How do you think this applies in other areas of prayer?
6. What does this passage show about the attitude of God to a sinful city? How do you think he views your city? What can you do about it?
7. The *Transformations* videos are mentioned in this chapter. Have you seen them? Do you think a similar prayer awakening and community transformation is possible in your country? What would it take to bring it about?

Chapter 7 – Desperate Prayer: The Story of Hannah

Text: 1 Samuel 1.

1. Hannah is faithful but sterile. Why did God allow this to happen?
2. Hannah turns her discouragement into prayer. What will help us to have this reaction too?
3. What areas of sterility are most evident in your church or in your own life?
4. Hannah is clearly emotional – weeping, not eating, 'pouring out her heart'. Is it good for prayer to be emotional? Why?
5. Hannah seems to align her will with God's as she promises to 'lend' her child to the Lord. Have you any experience of changing your motivation as you pray about an important subject?
6. Hannah has a 'secret history' with God. Do you? Spend some time discussing this and, if appropriate, give some personal testimony.
7. Hannah was accused of being drunk as she prayed. Is this a danger with you? How do you interpret this? Do you have any experience of it? Is this desirable in any way?
8. How do you think we should respond to those who accuse us of excess? Do we see the wise attitude of Hannah or another attitude among intercessors today? What can we do about it?
9. Talk about any answers to desperate prayer that any of your group may have had.

Chapter 8 – Fervent Prayer for a Nation: The Story of Joel

Text: Joel 2:1–32.
For Meditation: What will the 'Day of the Lord' be like for your nation?

1. Are you aware of the existence of a 'worldwide prayer movement'? Name some features that you observe in it.
2. Can you think of an event in your nation where God was calling people to repent?
3. How is the state of your nation, and how urgent is the need to repent? Why?
4. Have you had the experience of 'rending your heart' in prayer? Do you desire it? Could you describe it?
5. General Booth said, 'Try tears.' Have you tried them in prayer? With what result?
6. Discuss your experience of fasting. (Read Isaiah 58; Nehemiah 1; Acts 13:1–3.) Are you ready to add fasting to your 'prayer discipline' and fast for perhaps one day a week for a period? As a group, plan to fast together at some time.
7. Joel 2:13 speaks of the Lord who 'repents of evil'. How does this work? Is this an incentive to prayer?

Chapter 9 – Rebuilding the Family Prayer Altar

Texts: Joel 2:15–19; 28–32; Deuteronomy 6:1–15.

1. Do you feel that in your country the children and teenagers are in danger? Why?
2. Do you feel there is a 'spirit of prayer' falling on young people? Give examples.
3. In your experience, do couples and families pray together? If not, what prevents them?
4. What is your own practice? Are you satisfied with it?
5. In what way could your prayer life at home grow in quality and quantity?
6. Discuss what the application of this idea of building a family prayer altar could be for those who live alone. ('He sets the lonely in families.') How could it work in your church?

7. Ask the Holy Spirit to lead you and spend some moments reflecting on what you could change in the future in your practice of prayer as a family or extended family.
8. Share with others your decision, or your impression.

Chapter 10 – Praying for the Nations

Text: Isaiah 62.

1. Read Psalm 122. Spend some time considering what it means to 'pray for the peace of Jerusalem'.
2. 'For Jerusalem's sake I will not remain quiet' (Is 62:1). What do you think this means?
3. 'Your land will be called married.' Think of four or five examples of the meaning of this.
4. If you were a watchman guarding your city, what dangers would you see coming?
5. 'Removing the stones.' What is the most important of these?
6. What sins in our nation need confessing to God? Try to gain agreement as a group about this.
7. Do you think there is a 'redemptive calling' or 'prophetic destiny' for your nation? What is it?
8. Spend some time praying for these things.

Chapter 11 – Praying for the Church

Texts: Ephesians 6:10–end; Romans 8:22–27.

1. Which part of the armour of God do you think is the most important as you come to prayer?
2. What does it mean to pray 'in the Spirit'? Is this part of your prayer discipline? Could it be? How?
3. Do you 'pray at all times'? Describe your aspirations in this area.

4. Read Paul's prayer for the church at Ephesus in Ephesians 3. Experiment by writing a 'Pauline prayer' for your own church. Read it out, as you pray it to God.
5. 'Caught up in the third heaven' (2 Cor 12:9). Do you know what Paul is talking about? Taking care not to boast, describe what your experience is in this area.
6. Do you have a 'thorn in the flesh'? Reflect on whether God's strength is reflected in your weakness. How could it be more?
7. Spend some time praying for Israel, the Government, and for Christians, in the manner of Paul.
8. Do you have a 'passion for the church' like Paul? Describe your reaction to this idea.
9. Spend some time praying for the churches in your area.

Chapter 12 – Seven Prayer Burdens of Christ

Text: John 17:9–23.

1. What is the aspect of Jesus' prayer life that you most aspire to?
2. 'Go in to your Father in secret.' Consider what is your current practice of prayer alone. Are you satisfied with it? How could you improve? Be accountable in this area.
3. Spend some time praying for those you feel are in danger.
4. 'Being set apart for God.' Do you think this is a call for Christians today? In what way?
5. 'Trinity Unity.' Spend some time 'glorifying' or speaking well of the other churches in your town.
6. In your own church, how could you move more fully into this unity for which Christ prays?
7. Discuss your experience of seeing God's glory and pray for one another.
8. Jesus prays, 'Into your hands I commit my spirit.' Would

you say that you are ready for death? Discuss and reflect on what is not yet in place in your life. Pray for any who may be in the 'fear of death'.

Chapter 13 – When God Is Silent

Text: Habakkuk 1:1–4; 2:1–4; 3:1–6, 17–19.

1. Reflect on an area in your life where God has not yet answered prayer.
2. Do you identify with Habakkuk? In what way?
3. Reflect on whether you are able to 'wait for the Lord'. Discuss what has helped you in this area of your life.
4. Reflect on how you might grow in the area of worshipping in times of barrenness.
5. What is your reaction to Janis Chevreau's testimony?
6. Bring an area of unanswered prayer in your life to God and try to imitate Habakkuk's practice of questioning, seeing, remembering, waiting, worshipping.
7. Discuss and list the most important things you have learnt from this study of *The Discipline of Intimacy*. May God bless you in your walk with him.

The Prayer Principles *series*

When I Can't Pray by Rob Frost

Praying isn't always easy. There is much in life to throw us off course and keep us from developing regular communication with God. Rob Frost provides food for thought and prayer for up to four weeks of daily meditations. The result is a celebration of the most rewarding relationship we can have.

Learning the Joy of Prayer by Larry Lea

Praying to the Sovereign Lord of the universe is our duty – a privilege, even. But can regular prayer be a time of great *joy* as well? Larry Lea guides us through the Lord's Prayer, as we rediscover what it means to see 'his kingdom come' in our lives.

Renewing Your Prayer Life by Sue Barnett

Prayer is about relationships, not rules. Rather than giving a string of formulas for more effective praying, Sue Barnett focuses our attention on the One who both inspires and receives prayer.

How to Pray When He Doesn't Believe by Mo Tizzard

A personal and touching story of how one woman's faithfulness in prayer brought her husband to the Lord, through seemingly impossible circumstances.